7-32

THE HOLOCAUST

Selected Documents in Eighteen Volumes

John Mendelsohn
EDITOR

Donald S. Detwiler
ADVISORY EDITOR

A GARLAND SERIES

CONTENTS OF THE SERIES

THE HOLOCAUST

1. Legalizing the Holocaust
The Early Phase, 1933– 1939

Introduction by
John Mendelsohn

GARLAND PUBLISHING, INC.
NEW YORK • LONDON
1982

These documents have been reproduced from copies in
the National Archives. Dr. Mendelsohn's work was carried out entirely on his own time and without endorse-
ment or official participation by the National Archives as
an agency.

Library of Congress Cataloging in Publication Data
Main entry under title:

Legalizing the Holocaust, the early phase, 1933–1939.

(The Holocaust ; 1)
1. Jews—Legal status, laws, etc.—Germany—History—Sources.
I. Mendelsohn, John, 1928–   . II. Series.
D810.J4H655   vol. 1   940.53′15′03924s [342.43′ 0873]   81-80309
[KK928]   940.53′15′03924s [344.302873]
ISBN 0-8240-4875-X

Design by Jonathan Billing

The volumes in this series have been printed on acid-free,
250-year-life paper.

Printed in the United States of America

ACKNOWLEDGMENTS

I owe a debt of gratitude to many people who aided me during various stages of preparing these eighteen volumes. Of these I would like to mention by name a few without whose generous efforts this publication would have been impossible. I would like to thank Donald B. Schewe of the Franklin D. Roosevelt Library in Hyde Park, New York, for his speedy and effective help. Sally Marcks and Richard Gould of the Diplomatic Branch of the National Archives in Washington, D.C., extended help beyond their normal archival duties, as did Timothy Mulligan and George Wagner from the Modern Military Branch. Edward J. McCarter in the Still Picture Branch helped a great deal. I would also like to thank my wife, Tish, for letting me spend my evenings during the past few years with these volumes rather than with her and our children, Michael and Lisa.

J. M.

INTRODUCTION
TO THE SERIES

"Holocaust," an ancient word for the consumption of a whole by fire, today denotes the Nazi persecution of the Jews, resulting in the extermination of some six million men, women, and children. The Holocaust is one of the few events that cannot be easily integrated into the flow of history. More than other historical events it has defied rational explanation, and further study is necessary before it can be more fully understood. The present collection represents a carefully selected documentary history of the persecution of the Jews that took place during the twelve years from the accession of Hitler in 1933 to the defeat of Nazi Germany in 1945. To complete the story, records of the Allied trials in the early postwar years of perpetrators of the Holocaust are also included.

The records of the Holocaust amount to many tons of documents. These have been collected in research centers in various countries, such as Yad Vashem in Jerusalem, the Centre de Documentation Juive Contemporaine in Paris, and the Leo Baeck Institute and the YIVO Institute for Jewish Research in New York City. One of the largest Holocaust collections in the world is preserved at an institution that does not specialize in records of the Holocaust: the United States National Archives administered by the National Archives and Records Service with headquarters in Washington, D.C. Its vast and eclectic collections of documents number in the billions of pages.

The facsimiles of documents of the Holocaust that are published in this eighteen-volume edition come entirely from the holdings of the National Archives. The documents selected are arranged both in rough chronological order and topically, beginning with the efforts to legalize discrimination against the Jews by the Nazis and ending with some of the most telling postwar trials pertaining to responsibility for the Holocaust.

The eighteen volumes of documents are divided into four sections. The first, "Planning and Preparation," consists of seven volumes. Volumes 1 and 2 are concerned with the legal process that made the Holocaust possible. There are examples of legislation that disenfranchised Jews and discriminated against them in various ways. These volumes document the methods used by the Nazi government in eliminating Jews from all important intellectual, political, and economic positions not only in Germany, but also in the countries that eventually fell within the power perimeter of the National Socialists. Volume 3 is devoted to the Crystal Night Pogrom. Herschel Grynszpan, a dissident Polish Jew, assassinated the third secretary of the German embassy in Paris, Ernst vom Rath, in November 1938. The Nazis used this event to instigate a huge pogrom, the *Reichskristallnacht*, or Crystal Night, Pogrom, resulting in the destruction of synagogues, the breaking of windows of Jewish shops (hence the name of the pogrom), the arrest and confinement of thousands of Jews in concentration camps, as well as the levy of a fine of a billion marks upon the German Jewish community. A discussion of the events by Nazi leaders under the chairmanship of Field Marshal Hermann Goering begins to outline some of the major features of the "Final Solution." Included is documentation on the foreign reaction to the pogrom and plans for a show trial of Grynszpan.

Propaganda and economic deprivation of Jews are the main focus of Volume 4. One of the characteristics of Nazi Germany was the unending dissemination of anti-Semitic propaganda. This propaganda was directed at all levels of the population, but most intensively at the Hitler Youth, the Nazi party, and paramilitary and military organizations. The SS largely recruited the executors of the Holocaust from these groups. Propaganda also prepared the grounds for "Aryanization"—outright or thinly veiled confiscation of Jewish property. This volume includes a propaganda pamphlet depicting Jews as world parasites, which was distributed to the German armed forces; the ritual murder issue of *Der Stuermer*, reports to the Department of State, including an anti-Jewish propaganda leaflet; interrogation transcripts of Alfred Rosenberg; and documents on the Aryanization or looting of Jewish property, particularly that of the Rothschild and Petchek families.

The final three volumes in the first section pertain to Jewish emigration from Germany. Several documents deal with the abortive conference at Evian-les-Bains in France, called by the United States in 1938 in order to facilitate the emigration of German Jews, and with the Intergovernmental Committee on Political Refugees, which resulted from the Evian conference. Numerous records pertain to the S.S. *St. Louis* affair that occurred a few months before the outbreak of World War II. Because of increased Nazi terror larger numbers of Jews had begun to emigrate. The Cuban director of immigration had sold many landing permits wholesale to the Hamburg America Line, which resold these permits to individual Jews. A shift in Cuban policies invalidated the permits, but the line failed to inform the passengers. Thus, when over nine hundred passengers arrived on the *St. Louis* at Havana, they were prevented from disembarking and were forced to return to Europe. For the moment, they were saved by the unselfish actions of France, Holland, Belgium, and Great Britain permitting the emigrants to stay in their respective territories. Other documents in these volumes deal with landing problems similar to those of the S.S. *St. Louis*, futile attempts to effect the emigration of five thousand Jewish children, and obstacles to Jewish emigration created by the Nazis.

The second section of this series, entitled "The Killing of the Jews," consists of six volumes. The first volume (Volume 8) pertains to the deportation of Jews first to ghettos in Poland and then to the extermination centers there. In time the Jews were sent directly to the extermination centers. By 1944 several million Jews had been deported, the first being the Jews of Stettin and Schneidemuehl in 1940 and the last the Jews of Hungary. Volume 8 also documents the deportation from other cities in Germany, Holland, Belgium, France, Norway, Slovakia, Croatia, Rumania, and Bulgaria, as well as the deportation of Jews from the Palatinate to Vichy France. The brutal conditions under which deportations were carried out are noted in various detailed records.

Other volumes in Section Two deal with medical experiments on Jewish concentration camp inmates, the *Einsatzgruppen*, or murder commandos, the Wannsee Protocol and related records, killings in the extermination camps, and the judicial system and the Jews in Nazi Germany. The killing of Jews and others by injection was first carried out in sanatoria and was described as euthanasia. These killings were continued in concentration camps together with various medical or pseudo-medical experiments in which human beings were used as guinea pigs. The documents in Volume 9 concentrate on euthanasia, on sterilization experiments, and on the skeleton collection. About one hundred Jews were selected, killed, and defleshed in order to obtain their skulls and skeletons for a collection at the University of Strassburg that was to document to succeeding generations that the "extinct" Jews were "subhuman."

Soviet Jews were executed by gassing vehicles or by firing squads whose targets were groups ranging from a few individuals to thousands of men, women, and children. The perpetrators of these mass murders, who allegedly killed a million persons (including some non-Jews) following the Nazi invasion of the Soviet Union, were organized into four special task forces called *Einsatzgruppen*. Volume 10 is devoted to the bloody forays of these murder commandos, including the mass killings at Babi Yar near Kiev, the Christmas Massacre at Simferopol, the attempts to destroy all traces of the executions by exhuming and burning the bodies, as well as the disguising of the killings as antipartisan activities. The descriptions of the killings are generally by the perpetrators themselves.

About six weeks after the Nazi invasion of the Soviet Union, Field Marshal Hermann Goering ordered Reinhard Heydrich, the dreaded chief of the Security Police, to make preparations for a "total solution" of the Jewish question in Nazi-dominated Europe. One of the results of this order was the conference Am Grossen Wannsee in Berlin on January 20, 1942. Members of a number of German government agencies attended the meeting at which the *Endloesung*, or "Final Solution," was discussed and outlined together wth related topics, such as the treatment of part Jews and a plan for shipping all Jews to Madagascar. Heydrich proposed that, with the aid of the agencies represented, the Jews were to be collected and deported to the east. These discussions are summarized in the Wannsee Protocol and related documents reproduced in both English and German. Also included is a 1944 report by the U.S. Office of Strategic Services in which two escapees describe what happened to the deported Jews in the Auschwitz concentration camp.

Systematic extermination of the Jews in the extermination centers was accomplished first by using exhaust gases from trucks or generators and later by using an insecticide called Zyklon B. Personal property of murdered Jews was disposed of in various ways. Watches were distributed to the German army; jewelry was transferred to state-owned pawn shops for sale in international and domestic markets. Clothing was distributed among various segments of the population. Hair of the murdered was used in stuffing mattresses, and dental gold was melted down into gold bars. Among the documents in Volume 12 in this section are descriptions of the methods of killing, as told by extermination camp commanders and others, as well as records of the distribution of the loot taken from the murdered.

The depravity of Nazi anti-Semitism is further illustrated by several court cases. For the most part, the documents reproduced in the second section concentrate on German court cases. Foremost are cases of "racial pollution," for example, the Katzenberger case in which a Jew was sentenced to death for alleged sexual relations with a gentile girl. Another case that demonstrates the degree to which the Nazi Ministry of Justice made anti-Semitic doctrine part of the judicial system is the "Jewish mother-milk case." A Jewish woman sold her milk to a German doctor. He in turn sold the milk to German mothers who could not themselves nurse their babies. When the case came before the court, it convicted the Jewish woman of fraud for misrepresenting her milk as fit for German infants.

At first few in the world community believed the extent and the brutality of the extermination of the Jews. Although the Nazis attempted to keep the killings secret, they never succeeded in doing so, and information was available from many sources soon after the extermination began. As the murders accelerated, attempts to extend relief and to stage rescue operations for the Jews increased, particularly after President Roosevelt created the War Refugee Board in January 1944. The three volumes of Section Three, entitled "Rescue Attempts," document these events.

Various groups did attempt to relieve the suffering of the Jews and also to rescue them—primarily, Jewish organizations and the War Refugee Board. Although the relief arrived too late for most and under the circumstances was not extensive, it did aid thousands of Jews. The facsimiles reproduced in the first volume of this section (Volume 14) pertain to the emigration of the owners of important industrial firms in Hungary in exchange for cession of their holdings to the SS, relief for the persecuted Jews of Transnistria in Rumania, activities of the War Refugee Board, and the unsuccessful attempts by Jewish organizations to persuade the U.S. War Department to bomb the extermination facilities at Auschwitz and railroad centers leading there from Hungary.

As the fortunes of war turned against the Germans, the Nazis were willing to trade Jewish lives for urgently needed commodities. They hoped also that negotiating only with the Western Allies might drive a wedge into the Grand Alliance. Nowhere was this more apparent than in Hungary and in the negotiations involving Joel Brand, an officer of the Assistance and Rescue Committee in Budapest. Brand went to Istanbul with the Nazi offer to spare the lives of a million Jews in return for ten thousand trucks (to be used only against the Russians) and a few other commodities. The British arrested Brand when he entered Syria from Turkey and denounced the truck deal; and the slaughter of Hungarian Jews continued. In addition to the Brand mission dossier, the facsimiles reproduced in Volume 14 include documentation on the work of the War Refugee Board in Hungary and the views of SS Colonel Kurt Becher on the Jewish situation in Hungary.

During the closing month of World War II, the Nazi leadership tried desperately to obtain supplies and made frantic efforts to disrupt the unity of the Allies. Individual high-ranking Nazis, moreover, tried to create a more favorable postwar image of themselves by arranging negotiations designed to alleviate some of the suffering that their regime had caused. Several of these negotiations were carried on in Switzerland. The records selected for reproduction in the last volume of this section (Volume 16) concern Saly Mayer, the Swiss representative of the American Joint Distribution Committee who conducted negotiations with SS Colonel Kurt Becher on the exchange of Jewish lives for goods, and former Federal Swiss Councillor Jean Marie Musy, who was able to negotiate the release of a trainload of Jews from Nazi Germany to Switzerland.

The final two volumes of the series comprise Section Four, entitled "Punishment." Much of the most important documentation of the Holocaust was assembled in connection with the postwar prosecution of its perpetrators. The only major United States trial that was devoted almost entirely to the Holocaust was the Ohlendorf, or *Einsatzgruppen*, case. Other cases, tried at Nuernberg, that dealt with important aspects of the Holocaust were the International Military Tribunal and the Brandt and Pohl cases. In the Brandt, or "medical," case a number of physicians and SS officers were tried for conducting various experiments on concentration camp inmates and for the killing of Jews to obtain their skeletons for a collection at the University of Strassburg. In the Pohl, or "concentration camp," case a group of SS officers were convicted for managing the concentration camps and for profiteering from inmate labor in SS enterprises. In the Ohlendorf case a number of commanders and members of *Einsatzgruppen* stood trial for killing an estimated one million men, women and children in the Soviet Union, mainly Jews.

United States military tribunals tried nearly two hundred war crime suspects at Nuernberg in twelve separate proceedings. The defendants were grouped either by type of crime or by organization. The last to be tried was the "ministries" or von Weizsaecker case, in which a United States military tribunal convicted a number of individuals of various offenses, particularly crimes related to the Holocaust. These crimes included participation in the planning and carrying out of the exterminations, complicity of German Foreign Ministry officials in the deportation of Jews from Nazi-controlled areas, and the cooperation of the German Finance Ministry and bank officials in the conversion of concentration camp loot, such as dental gold, to foreign exchange.

Each of the eighteen volumes in the series begins with an introduction written either by the editor or by other scholars whose knowledge of the subject matter well qualifies them to write in their field of expertise. The introductions provide historical orientation to those aspects of the Holocaust to which the documents in a volume relate as well as general information regarding the documentation reproduced. Each introduction is followed by a detailed table of contents, in which the listing of each document is accompanied by a note on its content and source.

The collection consists predominantly of materials generated at the time of the Holocaust—either by its perpetrators or by those engaged in attempts to provide relief or rescue to the victims of the Holocaust. Several volumes also include records created in the early postwar years for the Nuernberg Trials.

Many of the records published in this series, particularly those contained in the first seven volumes, grouped under the heading "Preparation and Planning," were taken from the central decimal file of the U.S. Department of State; others came from the Nuernberg Trials prosecution document collections or from captured German records, especially the records of the *Reichsfuehrer* of the SS and chief of the German Police, Heinrich Himmler, and the documents of the German Foreign Ministry. Many records reproduced in subsequent volumes in the series are also from the Nuernberg Trials prosecution collections, materials from the Office of Strategic Services and other United States agencies are included as well. The facsimiles of Section Three, entitled "Rescue Attempts," were mainly selected from the records of the War Refugee Board in the Franklin D. Roosevelt Library in Hyde Park, New York, a subdivision of the U.S. National Archives.

Wherever possible, the original document bearing on a given phase of the Holocaust was selected for reproduction. Often, however, the English translation was preferred because of better legibility; sometimes both the original and the translation are included. Less than one-third of the document pages appear in the original German. Over two-thirds of the records reproduced are in English. A good number of these are official working translations. A very few other records are presented in their original Dutch, French, or Spanish.

The documents in this series were selected for publication so that libraries would have an overall official record of the Holocaust. Although this collection includes only a selection of records in one institution, they reflect the major topical areas of the Holocaust. The Holocaust is one of the few unique historical events that has forced us to view humanity differently. It has resulted in a never ending search for the meaning of the tragic events from 1933 to 1945. This series of documents will serve its purpose if it leads to a more profound understanding of the Holocaust.

John Mendelsohn

CONTENTS
OF THE SERIES

xiv

Volume 2. *Legalizing the Holocaust: The Later Phase, 1939–1943*

Volume 3. The Crystal Night Pogrom

Volume 4. Propaganda and Aryanization, 1938–1944

Volume 8. Deportation of the Jews to the East: Stettin, 1940, to Hungary, 1944

Volume 9. Medical Experiments on Jewish Inmates of Concentration Camps

Volume 10. The Einsatzgruppen *or Murder Commandos*

Volume 11. The Wannsee Protocol and a 1944 Report on Auschwitz by the Office of Strategic Services

Volume 13. The Judicial System and the Jews in Nazi Germany

Volume 14. Relief and Rescue of Jews from Nazi Oppression, 1943–1945

Volume 15. Relief in Hungary and the Failure of the Joel Brand Mission

Dossier on the Joel Brand Mission

Volume 16. Rescue to Switzerland: The Musy and Saly Mayer Affairs

Dossier on the Saly Mayer Negotiations

xl

Volume 17. Punishing the Perpetrators of the Holocaust: The Brandt, Pohl, and Ohlendorf Cases

Volume 18. Punishing the Perpetrators of the Holocaust: The Ohlendorf and Von Weizsaecker Cases

INTRODUCTION

Perhaps the most consistently pursued and horrifyingly implemented policy of the Nazi regime in Germany was the persecution of the Jews. In fact, it is the deplorable treatment of the Jews that sets Nazi misdeeds apart from other crimes; without these persecutions Nazi crimes would not appear so different from other forms of crime. The energies and resources of numerous government agencies were devoted to the relentless anti-Jewish drive. The Nazi party and the paramilitary organizations (especially the SS) molested, beat, tortured, and eventually exterminated first Germany's and then Europe's Jews. The German Foreign Ministry, the Ministry of the Interior, and the Propaganda Ministry collaborated and led in the development of the policy of discrimination and ultimately extermination. Nazi loyalists, from the central to the local levels, vigorously implemented their work so that a hierarchy of horrors became the official policy. The Justice Ministry, the Ministry of the Interior, and the Chancellery, in particular, cooperated in drafting anti-Jewish decrees, directives, and bills. Thus these official agencies imparted to the persecution of the Jews in Nazi Germany a legality, which was reenforced between 1933 and 1943 by the enactment into law of a large number of these drafts and the passage of anti-Jewish decrees. These measures systematically reduced the Jewish citizens of Germany to second-rate alien status and in the end brought about the death of millions of European Jews.

Several factors were responsible for the Nazi penchant for legality in the regime's anti-Jewish policy. Persecution of Jews prescribed by law tended to justify these actions to the world as well as to the general populace. Legality also made it easier to obtain the cooperation of the German citizenry than a clandestine and illegal persecution policy would have. Thus legalizing these discriminatory actions was a shrewd move in view of the German respect for law that in many cases approached idolatry. On the surface, at least, it lent the measures the appearance of lawfulness. In addition, acting in accordance with statutes seemed to remove some of the responsibility from the individual who carried out the discrimination. And many individuals, indeed, involved themselves in the process of these persecutions and atrocities, often on a voluntary basis. The large-scale persecution and eventual extermination of hundred thousands of fully integrated Jews could not have been carried out without the cooperation of considerable numbers of individuals. The most commonly used defense by the accused at the Nuernberg and other war crimes trials after World War II was the claim that the

German soldiers pasting signs on windows of Jewish businesses.
National Archives Heinrich Hoffman Collection of Still Pictures 242-HB-734

defendants killed and tortured, exterminated and committed genocide only pursuant to superior orders.

The Nazi take-over of the German government in 1933 opened the floodgates for anti-Semitic bills that the Nazi members of the Weimar legislature had attempted in vain to get accepted into law under the Weimar Republic. The vast majority of these laws, decrees, and regulations dealt with removal of Jews from public offices and expropriation of their property. Removing Jews from public, economic, and cultural life enabled the Nazi government to fill important positions, as well as those in the lower echelons of the government bureaucracy, with persons loyal to the Nazi cause and filled party and private coffers with loot from indemnities imposed on Jews and Aryanizations. In the professions Jewish lawyers and physicians found their practices severely restricted, and Jewish artists and writers could no longer officially exercise their crafts. Without this prior process of legalizing persecution of the Jews, it is impossible to see how their eventual extermination could have been carried out as it was.

In order to document the legalization of the persecution of the Jews, this volume reproduces facsimiles of a number of these anti-Semitic laws and other documents in rough chronological sequence from 1933 to 1939. The selections come from the central decimal files of the U.S. Department of State, the Nuernberg Trials prosecution document series, and captured German documents in the National Archives of the United States.

Some facsimiles deal with restrictive disabilities imposed upon medical doctors and other members of the medical and legal professions. Others form the legal basis for the elimination of the Jews as factors in the German economy, particularly as a consequence of the *Reichskristallnacht,* or Crystal Night, Pogrom in November 1938. This pogrom followed the assassination of Ernst vom Rath, a minor diplomat at the German embassy in Paris, by Herschel Grynszpan, a Polish Jew. Subsequent legislation and directives subjected German Jewry to a capital levy, excluded them from various types of business enterprises, and forced on them expropriations called Aryanizations, that is, forced sales of Jewish properties, often to loyal Nazis, at a fraction of their actual value. Earlier, the Nuernberg laws had deprived Jews of their citizenship and made intercourse between Jews or half-Jews and Germans illegal. Foreign Jews living in Germany at times received less discriminatory treatment. This is illustrated by several regulations reproduced in this volume dealing with the property and treatment of Jewish citizens of the United States living in Germany.

As noted already, legalizing the persecution was the first step in the eventual extermination of millions of Jews and in that sense it made their killing possible. It made mass murder appear less criminal in the eyes of the murderers. It facilitated the murders in the slaughter houses. Thus the documents selected and reproduced in this volume illustrate the pernicious and unique process of legalizing large-scale discrimination against citizens in a modern industrialized nation.

John Mendelsohn

SOURCE ABBREVIATIONS
AND DESCRIPTIONS

Nuernberg Document

Records from five of the twenty-five Nuernberg Trials prosecution document series: the NG (Nuernberg Government) series, the NI (Nuernberg Industrialist) series, the NO (Nuernberg Organizations) series, the NOKW (Nuernberg Armed Forces High Command) series, and the PS (Paris-Storey) series. Also included are such Nuernberg Trials prosecution records as interviews, interrogations, and affidavits, excerpts from the transcripts of the proceedings, briefs, judgments, and sentences. These records were used by the prosecution staff of the International Military Tribunal at Nuernberg or the twelve United States military tribunals there, and they are part of National Archives Record Group 238, National Archives Collection of World War II War Crimes Records.

OSS

Reports by the Office of Strategic Services in National Archives Record Group 226.

SEA

Staff Evidence Analysis: a description of documents used by the Nuernberg prosecution staff. Although the SEA's tended to describe only the evidentiary parts of the documents in the summaries, they describe the document title, date, and sources quite accurately.

State CDF

Central Decimal File: records of the Department of State in National Archives Record Group 59, General Records of the Department of State.

T 120

Microfilm Publication T 120: records of the German foreign office received from the Department of State in Record Group 242, National Archives Collection of Foreign Records Seized, 1941–. The following citation system is used for National Archives

Microfilm Publications: The Microfilm Publication number followed by a slash, the roll number followed by a slash, and the frame number(s). For example, Document 1 in Volume I: T 120/4638/K325518—K325538.

T 175

Microfilm Publication T 175: records of the Reich leader of the SS and of the chief of the German police in Record Group 242.

U.S. Army and U.S. Air Force

Records relating to the attempts to cause the U.S. Army Air Force to bomb the extermination facilities at Auschwitz and the railroad center at Kaschau leading to Auschwitz, which are part of a variety of records groups and collections in the National Archives. Included are records of the United States Strategic Bombing Survey (Record Group 243), records of the War Refugee Board (Record Group 220), records of the Joint Chiefs of Staff, and other Army record collections.

War Refugee Board

Records of the War Refugee Board, located at the Franklin D. Roosevelt Library in Hyde Park, New York. They are part of National Archives Record Group 220, Records of Temporary Committees, Commissions and Boards. Included in this category are the papers of Myron C. Taylor and Ira Hirschmann.

CONTENTS

1

li

Notes

1. *Document 6.* The signatures in this dossier are by *Adolf Hitler*; his deputy, *Rudolf Hess*, who is still serving a life imprisonment sentence imposed by the International Military Tribunal at Nuernberg in 1946; *Wilhelm Frick*, German minister of the interior, who was hanged following his being sentenced to death at Nuernberg; *Wilhelm Stuckart*, deputy secretary in the Ministry of the Interior, sentenced to a minimal prison term because of ill health by a United States military tribunal at Nuernberg in the "ministries case"; *Hans Pfundtner*, also a deputy secretary in the Ministry of the Interior; *Franz Guertner*, German minister of justice, who died in 1941; and *Reinhardt*, deputy in the Reich Finance Ministry.

2. *Document 8.* The document was selected from a file maintained by the deputy secretary in the German Ministry of Education, Zschintzsch.

3. *Documents 9, 13, and 14.* The letters of transmittal, telegram and report in the document are signed by the American ambassador in Berlin, Hugh R. Wilson.

4. *Document 12.* This correspondence file of the German Ministries of Justice, Economics and the Interior was maintained in the German Ministry of Justice.

5. *Documents 16 and 18.* The letters of transmittal are signed by Prentiss Gilbert, the charge d'affaires ad interim at the American embassy in Berlin.

6. *Document 17.* The reports are signed by Guenther Joel, a public prosecutor in Hamm, Germany, who was later sentenced to ten years imprisonment by the United States military tribunal adjudicating the so-called justice case at Nuernberg in 1947.

7. *Documents 20 and 21.* The letters of transmittal are signed by Raymond H. Geist, American consul in Berlin.

Gesetzliche Massnahmen zur Lösung der Judenfrage.

1933.

K325518

Gesetz zur Wiederherstellung des Berufsbeamtentums.
Vom 7. April 1933 (RGBl. I S. 175).

Erste Verordnung zur Durchführung des Gesetzes zur
Wiederherstellung des Berufsbeamtentums.
Vom 11. April 1933 (RGBl. I S. 195).

Zweite Verordnung zur Durchführung des Berufsbeamten-
gesetzes.
Vom 4. Mai 1933 (RGBl. I S. 233).

Dritte Verordnung zur Durchführung des Gesetzes zur
Wiederherstellung des Berufsbeamtentums.
Vom 6. Mai 1933 (RGBl. I S. 245).

Preuss. Durchführungsbestimmungen zum Gesetz zur Wiederherstellung des Berufsbeamtentums.
Vom 7. April 1933.

Runderlass des Reichs- und Preussischen Ministers des
Inhern zgl. im Namen des Ministerpräsidenten und der
übrigen Staatsminister mit Ausnahme des Justizministers
vom 31. Mai 1933.
2 d 1366 X. (MBliV. I S. 619).

1. Verordnung zur Durchführung des Gesetzes über Ehrenämter in der sozialen Versicherung und der Reichsversor-
gung.
Vom 19. Mai 1933 (RGBl. I S. 283).

Zweite Verordnung zur Durchführung des Gesetzes über
Ehrenämter in der sozialen Versicherung und der Reichs-
versorgung.
Vom 23. Juni 1933 (RGBl. I S. 397).

Zweite Änderungs- und Ergänzungsverordnung zur Durchführung des Gesetzes zur Wiederherstellung des Berufsbeamtentums.
Vom 28. September 1933 (RGBl. I S. 679).

Gesetz zur Änderung von Vorschriften auf dem Gebiete des
allgemeinen Beamten-, des Besoldungs- und des Versor-
gungsrechts.
Vom 3o. Juni 1933 (RGBl. I S. 433).

Richtlinien zu § 1 a Abs. 3 des Reichsbeamtengesetzes
in der Fassung des Gesetzes vom 3o. Juni 1933 (RGBl. I
S. 433.)
Vom 8. August 1933 (RGBl. I S. 575).

Runderlass des Reichsministers des Innern vom 17. August
1933 betr. Nachweisung arischer Abstammung beim Eintritt
in das Gemeindebeamtenverhältnis. - IV. a. I. 1349
(MBliV. I S. 967).

Änderung der Personalordnung der Deutschen Reichsbahnge-
sellschaft.
(52.5o4 Po v.). November 193: - RMBl. 1933 S. 672).

Gesetz über die Zulassung zur Rechtsanwaltschaft.
Vom 7. April 1933 (RGBl. I S. 187).

Gesetz zur Änderung einiger Vorschriften der Rechtsan-
waltsordnung, der Zivilprozessordnung und des Arbeits-
gerichtsgesetzes vom 2o. Juli 1933 (RGBl. I S. 522).

Gesetz betreffend die Zulassung zur Patentanwaltschaft
und zur Rechtsanwaltschaft.
Vom 22. April 1933 (RGBl. I S. 217).

Erste Durchführungsverordnung zum Gesetz betreffend die
Zulassung zur Patentanwaltschaft und Rechtsanwaltschaft.
Vom 2o. Juli 1933 (PGBl. I S. 528).

Zweite Durchführungsverordnung zum Gesetz betreffend
die Zulassung zur Patentanwaltschaft und Rechtsanwaltschaft.
Vom 1. Oktober 1933 (RGBl. I S. 699).

Patentanwaltsgesetz.
Vom 28. September 193: (RGBl. I S. 669).

K325519

Gesetz über die Zulassung von Steuerberatern,
Vom 6. Mai 1933 (RGBl. I S. 257).

Runderlass des Finanzministers und des Ministers des
Innern vom 8. Juni 1933 - II. A. 1341 und IV. St. 6o2 -
betr. Zulassung von Steuerberatern (MBliV. 1933 S. 696).

Gesetz über die Zulassung als Verwaltungsrechtsrat.
Vom 12. Juni 1933 (PrGS. S. 2o9).

Verordnung über die Zulassung von Ärzten bei den Krankenkassen.
Vom 22. April 1933 (RGBl. I. S. 222).

Verordnung über die Zulassung der Kriegsteilnehmer zur
ärztlichen Tätigkeit bei den Krankenkassen.
Vom 9. September 1933 (RGBl. I S. 26o).

Runderlass des Ministers des Innern IV. W. 32o2/24.8.
vom 7. November 1933 betr. Ausschliessung nichtarischer

2

Ärzte von der ärztlichen Versorgung Hilfsbedürftiger
(MBliV. I S. 1335).

Verordnung über die Tätigkeit von Zahnärzten und Zahntechnikern bei den Krankenkassen.
Vom 2. Juni 1933 (RGBl. I S. 350).

Verordnung über die Beendigung der Tätigkeit von Ärzten, Zahnärzten und Zahntechnikern bei den Krankenkassen
vom 30. Juni 1933 (RGBl. I S. 423).

Vergebung von Apothekerkonzessionen.
RdErl.d.MdI. vom 26. Oktober 1933 - III a II 3580/33.-
(MBliV. II S. 509).

Gesetz gegen die Überfüllung deutscher Schulen und Hochschulen.
Vom 25. April 1933 (RGBl. I S. 225).

Schriftleitergesetz.
Vom 4. Oktober 1933 (RGBl. I S. 713).

Verordnung über das Inkrafttreten und die Durchführung des Schriftleitergesetzes.
Vom 19. Dezember 1933 (RGBl. I S. 1085).

Erste Verordnung zur Durchführung des Reichskulturkammergesetzes.
Vom 1. November 1933 (RGBl. I S. 797).

Vierte Verordnung über die Vorführung ausländischer Bildstreifen.
Vom 28. Juni 1933 (RMBl. 33 S. 351).

Reichserbhofgesetz.
Vom 29. September 1933 (RGBl. I S. 685).

K325520

Erste Durchführungsverordnung zum Reichserbhofgesetz, insbesondere über Einrichtung und Verfahren der Anerbenbehörden.
Vom 19. Oktober 1933 (RGBl. I S. 749).

Zweite Durchführungsverordnung zum Reichserbhofgesetz.
Vom 19. Dezember 1933 (RGBl. I S. 1096).

Gesetz gegen Missbrauche bei der Eheschliessung und bei der Annahme an Kindesstatt.
Vom 23. November 1933 (RGBl. I S. 980).

Gesetz über den Widerruf von Einbürgerungen und die Aberkennung der deutschen Staatsangehörigkeit vom 14. Juli 1933.

Reichskulturkammergesetz vom 22. September 1933

Ausführungsverordnung zum Schriftleitergesetz vom 19. Dezember 1933.

3

Reichsbeamtengesetz in der Fassung vom 3o. Juni 1933.
(RGBl. I S. 433).

Erste Verordnung zur Durchführung des Gesetzes gegen
die Überfüllung deutscher Schulen und Hochschulen vom 25.
April 1933 (RGBl. I S. 226).

Verordnung über die Zulassung von Ärzten zur Tätigkeit bei
den Krankenkassen vom 22. April 1933 (RGBl. I S. 222) in
der Fassung der Verordnung vom 2o. November 1933 (RGBl. I
S 983).

Verordnung über die Tätigkeit von Zahnärzten und Zahntechnikern bei den Krankenkassen vom 2. Juni 1933 (RGBl. I
S 35o) in der Fassung der Verordnung vom 2o. November 1933

Verordnung über die Zulassung von Zahnärzten und Zahntechnikern zur Tätigkeit bei/den Krankenkassen vom 27. Juli
1933 (RGBl. I S 541) in der Fassung der Verordnung vom
2o. November 1933 (RGBl. I S. 983).

Verordnung über die Zulassung von Ärzten, Zahnärzten
und Zahntechnikern zur Tätigkeit bei den Krankenkassen
vom 2o. November 1933. (RGBl. I S. 983).

4

1934.

Gesetz zur Änderung des Gesetzes zur Wiederherstellung
des Berufbeamtentums.
Vom 22. März 1934 (RGBl. I S. 2o3).

Runderlass des Preuss. Finanzministers zgl. im Namen des
Ministerpräsidenten und der übrigen Staatsminister.
Vom 14. April 1934 - I. C. 33o3/31. 3. (MBliV.1934 S.623).

Nachweis der arischen Abstammung bei der Prüfung kommunaler Ehrenbeamter.
RdErl. d. MdI. u.d. FM. vom 31. Oktober 1934 - IV a I
174/34 d. IV 711o/23. 8. 34. (MBliV. S. 144o).

Verordnung über die Zulassung von Ärzten zur Tätigkeit
bei den Krankenkassen.
Vom 17. Mai 1934 (RGBl. I S. 399).

Prüfungsordnung für Apotheker.
Vom 8. Dezember 1934 (RMBl. 1934 S. 769).

Erste Anordnung Nr. 18 der Reichstheaterkammer vom 3.
Mai 1934, betr. Anmeldung der Bühnenlehrer, abgedruckt
bei Schreiber, das Recht der Reichskulturkammer, Bd. I
S. 173 (Arische Abstammung der Hilfskräfte).

Zweite Anordnung Nr. 21 der Reichstheaterkammer vom 15.
Juni 1934, betr. Lehrtätigkeit für den Bühnenberuf, abgedruckt bei Schrieber, aaO., Bd. I S. 175 (Arische Abstammung der Bühnenlehrer und ihrer Hilfskräfte).

3. Anordnung Nr. 26 der Reichstheaterkammer, betr. Standes
ordnung für die deutschen Zanzlehrer, I. A. 1. Erforder-
nis der arischen Abstammung für die Zulassung zur Reichs-
fachprüfung (V.S. 34/7.8.; Schrieber, aaO. I S 185).

Änderung von Familien- und Vornamen.
RdErl. d. MdI. v. 25. Juni 1934 - I. Z. 1o. IV.
(MBliV. 1934 S. 885).

Erlass über den Ausschluss der im nichtarischen Besitz
befindlichen Apotheken von Wohlfahrtslieferungen
RMBliV. 1934, Seite 1125).

Staatliche Anerkennung als Volkspfleger.
Rd.Erl. U. II. M 14o9 U. II. G. des M.f.Wiss., . u. V.
vom 2. August 1934 (Zentralbl. f.d.g. Unter.Verw.Pr.
1934 S. 247).

Gutachten über arische Abstammung.
RdErl. d. RMI. vom 26. Oktober 1934 - IV 5o1 8 b 15. 8.
(MBliV. S. 1416).

Zweite Verodnung zur Durchführung des Gesetzes zur Wiederherstellung des Berufsbeamtentums vom 4. Mai 1933 (RGBl.
I S. 233) in der Fassung der Verordnungen vom 7. Juli 1933
(RGBl. I S. 458), vom 28. September 1933 (RGBl. I S. 678)
und vom 7. Mai 1934 (RGBl. I S. 373).

5

Erläuterung des Reichsministers der Finanzen zum Gesetz
über Förderung der Eheschließungen vom 5. Juli 1933
und 22. August 1933 in der Fassung vom 7. März 1934.
(Deutscher Reichsanzeiger und Preussischer Staats-
anzeiger vom 31. März 1934 Nr. 76).

6

1935.

Reichsbürgergesetz.
Vom 15. September 1935 (RGBl. I S. 1146).

Gesetz zum Schutze des deutschen Blutes und der deutschen Ehre.
Vom 15. September 1935 (RGBl. I S. 1146).

1. Verordnung zum Reichsbürgergesetz.
Vom 14. November 1935 (RGBl. I S. 1333).

1. Verordnung zur Ausführung des Gesetzes zum Schutze des deutschen Blutes und der deutschen Ehre.
Vom 14. November 1935 (RGBl. I S. 1334).

Verbot von Rassenmischehen.
RdErl. d. RuPrMdI. vom 26. November 1935 - I B 3/324 II
(MBliV. S. 1429).

Bekanntmachung.
Vom 21. November 1935 bzgl. des § 3 des Gesetzes zum Schutze des deutschen Blutes und der deutschen Ehre.
(RMBl. 1935, S. 835).

Befreiungen von den Vorschriften des Reichsbürgergesetzes und des Blutschutzgesetzes sowie der Ausführungsverordnung hierzu.
RdErl. des RuPrMdI vom 4. Dezember 1935 - I B 3/416.
(MBliV. S. 1455).

Übertritt der jüdischen Beamten in den Ruhestand.
RdErl. d. RuPrMdI. vom 9. Dezember 1935 - II SB 61co/43o
(MBliV. Nr. 52).

Übertritt der jüdischen Beamten in den Ruhestand.
RdErl.d.RuPrMdI. vom 2o. Dezember 1935 - II SB 61oo/9o1.
(MBliV. S. 15o4).

Ausscheiden der jüdischen Träger eines öffentlichen Amtes.
RdErl. d. RuPrMdI. zgl. i. N. samtl. RM., d. PrMPräs. u. samtl. PrStM vom 21. Dezember 1935 - I A 16 234/5o16 II.
(MBliV. S 15o6).

Zweite Verordnung zum Reichsbürgergesetz.
Vom 21. Dezember 1935 (RGBl. I S. 1524).

Ausführungsanweisung zu § 3 der 1. Verordnung zur Ausführung des Gesetzes zum Schutze des deutschen Blutes und der deutschen Ehre.
RdErl. d. RuPrMdI. zgl. i. N. StdF vom 23. Dezember 1935
- I G 4 Allg./1oco. (RMBliV 1936 S. 11).

Durchführung des Gesetzes zum Schutze des deutschen
Blutes und der deutschen Ehre vom 15. September 1935
(RGBl. I S. 1146) und des Gesetzes zum Schutze der Erbge-
sundheit des deutschen Volkes (Ehegesundheitsgesetz)
vom 18. Oktober 1935 (RGBl. I S. 1246).

Nachweis der arischen Abstammung von Notaren und
Notarvertretern.
AV. des RIM. vom 2h. November 1935 (Ia 1318).
- Deutsche Justiz S. 1688. -

Reichsärzteordnung.
Vom 13. Dezember 1935 (RGBl. I S. 1433).

Artikel 7 der 4. Ausführungsverordnung des Gesetzes zur
Verhütung erbkranken Nachwuchses vom 18. Juli 1935.
(RGBl. I S. 1o35.)

Vierte Verordnung über die Zulassung von Zahnärzten und
Dentisten zur Tätigkeit bei den Krankenkassen.
Vom 9. Mai 1935 (RGBl. I S. 594).

Ariernachweis der Kandidaten der Pharmazie.
RdErl. d. RuPrMdI. vom 28. Oktober 1935 - IV 3 1o2o3/36o5
(MBliV. S. 1341).

Verordnung über das Erfassungswesen .
Vom 7. November 1935 (RGBl. I S. 1927).

Verordnung über die Musterung und Aushebung vom 21. März
1935 (RGBl. I S. 2o1).

Verordnung über die Zulassung von Nichtariern zum aktiven
Wehrdienst.
Vom 25. Juli 1935 (RGBl. I S. 1o47).

Reichsarbeitsdienstgesetz.   K325525
Vom 26. Juni 1935 (RGBl. I S. 769).

Zweite Verordnung zur Durchführung und Ergänzung des
Reichsarbeitsdienstgesetzes.
Vom 1. Oktober 1935 (RGBl. I S. 1215).

Anordnung zur Wahrung der Unabhängigkeit des Zeitungs-
verlagswesens.
Vom 24. April 1935 (B.B. 35/25. 4.).

Aufnahmebestimmungen für die Reichsschaft der Studieren-
den an den deutschen Hoch- und Fachschulen.
RdErl. d. RuPrMdWEV. vom 6. Juli 1935 - W. I. i 1736).
(RMinAmtsblDtschWiss. 1935 S. 311).

Dritte Änderung der "Richtlinien für das Strafverfahren"
und der "Mitteilungen in Strafsachen".
AV.d.RIM. vom 17. Dezember 1935 (III a 19844/35.).
Deutsche Justiz S. 1854.

Auswahl von Ar,enanwälten, Pflichtverteidigern,
Konkurswaltern und dergl.
AV. d. RIM. vom 19. Dezember 1935 (IV b 8o4o).-
Deutsche Justiz S. 1858.

Judenverordnung der Deutschen Rechtsfront vom 2. Sep-
temner 1935, abgedruckt im Mitteilungsblatt des NSRB.

Verordnung zur Ausführung des Gesetzes zur Verhütung
von Missbrauchen auf dem Gebiete der Rechtsberatung.
Vom 13. Dezember 1935 (RGBl. I S. 1481)

Mitwirkung der Srandesbeamten bei Eheschliessungen ~~zwish~~
zwischen Ariern und Nichtariern.
RdErl. d. RuPrMdI. vom 26. Juli 1935 - I B 3/195.

Runderlass zum Blutschutzgesetz.
RdErl. d. RuPrMdI vom 26. November 1935 - I B 3/324 II.

Ergänzung der Ausführungsanweisung zu § 3 der ersten
Verordnung zur Ausführung des Gesetzes zum Schutze des
deutschen Blutes und der deutschen Ehre vom 23. Dezem-
ber 1935.
RdErl. d. RuPrMdI. zgl. i.N.d.StdF. vom 24. März 1936
I G 19 Allg./1ooo.

Beschaffung von Urkunden zum Nachweise der arischen Ab-
stammung aus dem Auslande.
RdErl. d. RuPrMdI. vom 24. September 1935 - I B 3. 179
II/III.

Gebührenfreiheit bei der Ausstellung von Urkunden zum
Nachweise der arischen Abstammung.
RdErl. d. RuPrMdI. vom 1o. Oktober 1935 - I B 3/3o5.

Begriff "Mischehe"
RdErl. d. RuPrMdI. vom 26. April 1935 - IV f 1814/1o75 c.

Ahnenpass
RdErl. d.RuPrMdI. vom 26. Januar 1935 - I B 22/236 II.

Gebührenfreiheit bei der Ausstellung von Urkunden zum
Nachweis der arischen Abstammung
RdErl. d.RuPrMdI vom 4. Marz 1935 - I B 3/29.

Drotte Verordnung über die Zulassung von ~ahnärzten und
Dentisten zur Tätigkeit bei den Krankenkkassen vom 13.
Februar 1935 (RGBl. I S. 192).

Vierte Verordnung zur Durchführung des Gesetzes über
Ehrenämter in de sozialen Versicherung und der Reichs-
versorgung (Vertretung gegenüber Versicherungsträgern
und Versicherungsbehörden in der Reichsversicherung) vom
9. September 1935 (RGBl. I S. 1143).

Vierte Verordnung zur Ausführung des Gesetzes zur Verhütung erbkranken Nachwuchses vom 18. Juli 1935 (RGBl. I
S 1o35).

1936.

Reichsausschuss zum Schutze des deutschen Blutes.
RdErl.d.RuPrMdI. zgl. i.N. d. StdF. vom 17. Januar 1936 -
I G 7 Allg./1ooo (RMBliV. S. 135).

Verordnung über die Flaggenführung der Schiffe.
Vom 17. Januar 1936 (RGBl. I S. 15.)

Verordnung über die Rechtsverhältnisse der Angehörigen
der Landespolizei.
Vom 7. Januar 1936 (RGBl. I S. 8).

Gesetz über das Reichstagswahlrecht.
Vom 7. März 1936 (RGBl. I S. 133).

Erste Verordnung zur Reichstagswahl.
Vom 7. März 1936 (RGBl. I S. 134).

Gewährung von Unterhaltszuschüssen, Festsetzung und
Verrechnung der Versorgungsbezüge für die am 1.1.1936 in
den Ruhestand getretenen jüdischen Beamten.
RdErl.d.RuPrMdI. vom 4. Mai 1936.- Va 255o/36.- (MBliV.
S. 613).

Reichstierärzteordnung.   K325527
Vom 3. April 1936 (RGBl.I S. 347).

Verordnung über die Musterung und Aushebung.
Vom 31. März 1936 (RGBl. I S. 2o1).

Verordnung zur Durchführung des § 1o7 a der Reichsabgaben-
ordnung.
Vom 11. Januar 1936 (RGBl. I S. 11).

Erste Verordnung zum Gesetz über die Verpachtung und Verwaltung öffentlicher Apotheken.
Vom 26. März 1936 (RGBl. I S. 317).

Gesetz über die Befähigung zum höheren bautechnischen
Verwaltungsdienst.
Vom 16. Juli 1936 (RGBl. I S. 563).

Ausführungsverordnung des Reichsinnenministers v
Vom 4. Februar 1936 - IV b 56 (Deutsche Justiz S. 2o8).
 Durchführung des Gesetzes zum Schutze des deutschen
Blutes und der deutschen Ehre vom 15. September 1935 (RG
Bl. I S. 1146) und des Gesetzes zum Schutze der Erbge-
sundheit des deutschen Volkes (Ehegesundheitsgesetz) vom
18. Oktober 1935 (RGBl. I S. 1246).

Gesetz zur Änderung des Wehrgesetzes.
Vom 26. Juni 1936 (RGBl.I S. 518).

Verordnung über das Heiraten der Angehörigen der Wehr-
macht.
Vom 1. April 1936 (Heiratsordnung, Heeresverordnungsbl.
S 121).

Ausführungsbestimmungen zur Heiratsordnung.
(heeresverordnungsblatt S. 123).

11

K325528

Erlass des Reichsministers der Finanzen betr. Kinderbeihilfen an kinderreiche Familien.
Vom 18. November 1936 (N 2o74 - 7o II).

Inanspruchnahme der Reichsstelle für Sippenforschung
bei Abstammungsprüfungen.
RdErl. d. RuPrMdI. vom 6. Juli 1936 - I A 4619/5o18^b.

Verordnung über die geschäftsmässige Hilfeleistung
in Devisensachen.
Vom 29. Juni 1936 (RGBl. I S. 524).

Versagung von Notstandbeihilfen bei Inanspruchnahme
jüdischer Ärzte.
RdErl. d. RuPrMdI. zgl. i. N. sämtl. RMi, d.PrMiPräs.
u. sämtl.PrSTM. vom 9. Oktober 1936 - II SB 64o3/46o8 -.

~~Kindesannahmeverfahren~~
~~RdErl. d. RuPrMdI. vom 6. xx.tygsatx~~

Anordnung des Präsidenten der Reichspressekammer vom
15. April 1936 bzgl. des Abstammungsnachweises der Mitglieder der Reichspressekammer.

Anordnung des Reichsleiters der DAF vom 11. Januar 1936
bzgl. der Mitgliedschaft zur DAF.

Erlass des Reichsinnenministers vom 29. Juni 1936 ~~bzgl.~~
Jüdische Geschäfte werden als Annahmestellen zur Entge-
gennahme von Bedarfsdeckungsscheinen nicht zugelassen.
~~Ebenso box gibt für die Zulassung zur Annahme von Fahr-
fahrzgutscheinen und von Fettverbilligungsscheinen.~~

Nachprüfung der Abstammung von Schiedsmännern.
AV. d.RMI vom 8. Oktober 1936 (318o - I a 1o818).-
Deutsche Justiz S. 1551-,

Arische Abstammung des zukünftigen Ehegatten und Heirats-
anzeige.
AV. d. RIM. vom 13. Oktober 1936 (2o4o - I.a 1o741).
Deutsche Justiz S. 1592.

Reichsausschuss zum Schutze des deutschen Blutes.
RdErl. d. RuPrMdI., zgl. i.N. d. StdF. vom 17. Januar
1936 - IGS 7 Allg./1ooo.

1937.

Deutsches Beamtengesetz.
Vom 26. Januar 1937 (RGBl. I S. 39).

Reichsnotarordnung.
Vom 13. Februar 1937 (RGBl. I S. 191).

Verordnung über das Erfassungswesen.
Vom 15. Februar 1937 (RGBl. I S. 2o5).

Gesetz zur Änderung des Reichsarbeitsdienstgesetzes.
Vom 19. März 1937 (RGBl. I S. 325).

Verordnung über die Musterung und Aushebung.
Vom 17. April 1937 (RGBl. I S. 469).

Verordnung über die Heranziehung der deutschen
Staatsangehörigen im Ausland zum aktiven Wehrdienst
und zum Reichsarbeitsdienst.
Vom 17. April 1937 (RGBl. I S. 517).

Erste Durchführungsverordnung zum Luftschutzgesetz.
Vom 4. Mai 1937 (RGBl. I S. 559).

Deutsches Polizeibeamtengesetz.
Vom 24. Juni 1937 (RGBl. I S. 653).
(§ 2 des deutschen Polizeibeamtengesetzes verweist auf
die allgemein geltenden reichsrechtlichen Vorschriften,
d.h. also auch auf § 25 des deutschen Beamtengesetzes).

Verordnung zur Durchführung des Deutschen Beamtengesetzes.
Vom 29. Juni 1937 (RGBl. I S 669).

Gesetz über Massnahmen im ehemaligen oberschlesischen
Abstimmungsgebiet.
Vom 3o. Juni 1937 (RGBL. I S. 717).

Dritte Verordnung über die Zulassung von Ärzten
zur Tätigkeit bei den Krankenkassen.
Vom 8. September 1937 (RGBl. I S. 973).

Bekanntmachung der neuen Fassung der Verordnung über
die Zulassung von Ärzten zur Tätigkeit bei den Krankenkassen (Zulassungsordnung für Ärzte).
Vom 8. September 1937 (RGBl. I S. 977).

Sechste Durchführungsbestimmungen zur Verordnung über
die Gewährung von Kinderbeihilfen an kinderreiche Familien.
Vom 31. August 1937 (RGBl. I S. 989).

Gesetz über die Durchführung einer Volks-, Berufs-
und Betriebszählung.
Vom 4. Oktober 1937 (RGBl. I S. 1o53).

13

Bestallungsordnung für Apotheker.
Vom 8. Oktober 1937 (RGBl. I S. 1118).

Gesetz über erbrechtliche Beschränkungen wegen gemein-
schaftswidrigen Verhaltens.
Vom 5. November 1937 (RGBl. I S. 1161).

Verordnung über die Ausbildung und Prüfung für den höheren vermessungstechnischen Verwaltungsdienst.
Vom 3. November 1937 (RGBl. I S. 1165).

Anord.ung des Sonderbeauftragten des Reichsministers
für Volksaufklarung und Propaganda vom 3o. Juli 1937
bzgl. der Herausgabe von Büchern und Broschüren durch
Juden.

Richtlinien des Reichsministers für Wissenschaft, Erziehung und Volksbildung vom 2. Juli 1937 über die Rechtsstellung der Juden im deutschen Schulwesen.

Erlass des Reichswirtschaftsministers bzgl. der Stellung
der Juden in der Organisation der gewerblichen Wirtschaft.
Vom 24. Dezember 37 (IV. 32164/37.)

Anordnung des Reichswirtschaftsministers betr. die Neu-
errichtung von Betrieben oder Unternehmen der Wirtschafts-
gruppe Bekleidungsindustrie in Berlin im Dezember 1937
(2 Pr. 22615/37).

Erlass des Reichsministers für Wissenschaft, Erziehung
und Volksbildung vom 29. Oktober 1937 (E. II e Nr. 2lo7
M.) bzgl. der Richtlinien zur Aufstellung von Lehrplä-
nen für jüdische Volksschulen.

Erlass des Reichs- und Preussischen Ministers für Wis-
senscgaft, Erziehung und Volksbildung vom 2. Juli 1937
bzgl. der Zulassung zur Ablegung der wissenschaftlichen
Prüfung für das höhere Lehramt, zur Prüfung für das
Handelslehramt und für das künstlerische Lehramt.

Anordnung des Reichsministers für Volksaufklarung und
Propaganda vom 15. Juli 1937 - Richtlinien für das jüdische Pressewesen -.

Erlass des Preussischen Finanzministers und des Reichsministers des Innern vom il. Juni 1937 bzgl. der jüdischen milden Stiftungen.

Bekanntmachung der Reichsrechtsanwaltskammer vom
23. Februar 1937 bzg. der Ausbildung von Lehrlingen
bei jüdischen Rechtsanwälten.

K325531

Runderlass des Reichsministers des Innern betr. weiterer Ausführungsanweisungen zur Durchführung der deutschen Gemeindeordnung "Juden nicht mehr Gemeindebürger".
Vom 31. Marz 1937 - V a VI 7. 17o III - 36. (RMiBl. 1937, Nr. 14 S. 518).

Berufsschutzanordnung des Präsidenten der Reichspressekammer bzgl. des werbenden Zeitschriftenhandels, der Lesezirkel, des Zeitungs- und Zeitschriftengrossvertriebs und des Bahnhofbuchhandels.
Vom 21. April 1937.

Berufsschutzanordnung des Präsidenten der Reichspressekammer für den Zeitungen- und Zeitschrifteneinzelhandel.
Vom 21. April 1938.

~~Rundverfügung des Oberbürgermeisters der Reichshauptstadt Berlin über die fachärztliche Versorgung~~

Kindesannahmeverfahren.
RdErl. d. RuPrMdI. vom 6. August 1937 - I B[1] 3/412 V 35.

K325532

1938.

Gesetz über die Änderung von Familien- und Vornamen.
Vom 5. Januar 1938 (RGBl. I S. 9).

Erste Verordnung zur Durchführung des Gesetzes über
die Änderung von Familiennamen und Vornamen.
Vom 7. Januar 1938 (RGBl. I S. 12).

Fünfte Verordnung über die Zulassung von Zahnärzten
und Dentisten zur Tätigkeit bei den Krankenkassen.
Vom 12. Januar 1938 (RGBl. I S. 29).

Viertes Gesetz zur Änderung über das Versteigerergewerbe.
Vom 5. Februar 1938 (RGBl. I S 115).

Gesetz zur Änderung des Einkommensteuergesetzes.
Vom 1. Februar 1938 (RGBl. I S. 99).

Bekanntmachung der neuen Fassung des Einkommensteuergesetzes.
Vom 6. Februar 1938 (RGBl. I S. 121).

Zweite Verordnung zur Durchführung des Steuerabzugs
vom Arbeitslohn - Zweite Lohnsteuerdurchführungsverordnung -.
Vom 1o. Februar 1938 (RGBl. I S. 149).

Bekanntmachung der neuen Fassung des Gesetzes über das
Versteigerergewerbe.
Vom 12. Februar 1938 (RGBl. I S. 2o2).

Erlass des Führers und Reichskanzlers über die Vereidigung der Beamten des Landes Österreich.
Vom 15. März 1938 (RGBl. I S. 245).

Erster Erlass des Führers und Reichskanzlers über die
Einführung deutscher Reichsgesetze in Österreich.
Vom 15. März 1938 (RGBl. I S. 247).

Erste Verordnung zur Volksabstimmung und zur Wahl des
Grossdeutschen Reichstag.
Vom 22. März 1938 (RGBl. I S. 289).

Gesetz über die Rechtsverhältnisse der jüdischen Kultusvereinigungen.
Vom 28. März 1938 (RGBl. I S. 338).

Verordnung über Angelegenheiten der Rechtsanwalte, Verteidiger, Notare und Patentanwälte in Österreich.
Vom 31. März 1938 (RGBl. I S. 353).

Gesetz über die Änderung und Ergänzung familienrechtlicher Vorschriften und über die Rechtsstellung der
Staatenlosen.
Vom 12. April 1938 (RGBl. I S. 38o). K325533

16

~~Verordnung über die Anmeldung des Vermögens von Juden.~~
Vom 26. April 1938 (RGBl. I S. 414).

Anordnung auf Grund der Verordnung über die Anmeldung
des Vermögens von Juden.
Vom 26. April 1938 (RGBl. I S. 415).

Verordnung zur Durchführung des Gesetzes über die
Änderung und Ergänzung familienrechtlicher Vorschriften
und über die Rechtsstellung der Staatenlosen.
Vom 23. April 1938 (RGBl. I S. 417).

Allgemeine Dienstordnung (ADO.) für nicht beamtete Gefolgschaftsmitglieder bei öffentlichen Verwaltungen und
Betrieben, insbesondere zur Allgemeinen Tarifordnung
für Gefolgschaftsmitglieder im öffentlichen Dienst (ATO).
Vom 3o. April 1938 (RGBl. I S. 461).

Erste Verordnung zur Ausführung des Personenstandsge-
setzes.
Vom 19. Mai 1938 (RGBl. I S. 533).

Zweite Verordnung über Angelegenheiten der Rechtsanwälte
und Notare im Lande Österreich.
Vom 11. Juni 1938 (RGBl. I S. 622).

~~Verordnung über die Einführung der Gesetze über Wirt-
schaftswerbung~~

Verordnung über die Einführung der Reichskulturkammerge-
setzgebung im Lande Österreich.
Vom 11. Juni 1938 (RGBl. I S. 624).

Dritte Verordnung zum Reichsbürgergesetz.
Vom 14. Juni 1938 (RGBl. I S. 627).

Verordnung über die Einführung des Schriftleitergesetzes
im Lande Österreich.
Vom 14. Juni 1938 (RGBl. I S. 629).

Verordnung über die Einführung von Wehrrecht im Lande
Österreich.
Vom 15. Juni 1938 (RGBl. I S. 631).

Verordnung zur Änderung der Verordnung zur Neuordnung
des österreichischen Berufsbeamtentums.
Vom 15. Juni 1938 (RGBl. I S. 643).

Verordnung über die deutsche Staatsangehörigkeit im
Lande Österreich.
Vom 3. Juli 1938 (RGBl. I S. 79o).

Verordnung über die Einführung des Personenstandsrechts
im Lande Österreich.
Vom 2. Juli 1938 (RGBl. I S. 8o3).

17

K325534

Gesetz zur Änderung der Gewerbeordnung für das
Deutsche Reich.
Vom 6. Juli 1938 (RGBl. I S. 823).

Verordnung über Kennkarten.
Vom 22. Juli 1938 (RGBl. I S. 913).

Dritte Bekanntmachung über den Kennkartenzwang.
Vom 23. Juli 1938 (RGBl. I S. 922).

Verordnung über die Einführung des rbhofrechts im
Lande Österreich (ÖEHV).
Vom 7. Juli 1938 (RGBl. I S. 935).

Vierte Verordnung zum Reichsbürgergesetz.
Vom 25.Juli 1938 (RGBl. I S. 969).

Verordnung über die Überprüfung und Ergänzung der
Schöffenlisten im Lande Österreich.
Vom 6. Juli 1938 (RGBl. I S. 879).

Gesetz über eine Bereinigung alter Schulden.
Vom 17. August 1938 (RGBl. I S. 1033).

Zweite Verordnung zur Durchführung des Gesetzes über
die Änderung von Familiennamen und Vornamen.
Vom 17. August 1938 (RGBl. I S. 1044).

Ausländerpolizeiverordnung.
Vom 22. August 1938 (RGBl. I S. 1053).

Gesetz über die Zulassung zur Patentanwaltschaft.
Vom 4. September 1938 (RGBl. I S. 1150).

Verordnung über die Einführung reichsrechtlicher Vor-
schriften auf dem Gebiete des Beamtenrechts im Lande
Österreich.
Vom 28. September 1938 (RGBl. I S. 1225).

Verordnung über Reisepässe von Juden.
Vom 5. Oktober 1938 (RGBl. I S. 1342).

Verordnung gegen die Unterstützung der Tarnung jüdischer
Gewerbebetriebe vom 22. April 1938 (RGBl. I S. 404).

Verordnung zur Durchführung der Verordnung über die
Anmeldung des Vermögens von Juden.
Vom 28. Juni 1938 (RGBl. I S. 640).

Gesetz zum Schutz der österreichischen Wirtschaft vom
14. Juni 1938 (RGBl. I S. 145).

Österreichisches Gesetz über die Bestellung von
kommissarischen Verwaltern und kommissarischen Über-
wachungspersonen.
Vom 17. Juni 1938.

K325535

Erlass des Reichswirtschaftsministers vom 5. Juli 1938
über die Durchführung der auf Grund der Verordnung über
die Anmeldung des Vermögens von Juden erlassenen Anordnung des Beauftragten für den Vierjahresplan. - III Jd
2818/38.-

Erlass des Reichswirtschaftsministers vom 5. August 1938
betr. Verausserung jüdischer Gewerbebetriebe. - III Jd
4114/38.-

Erlass des Reichswirtschaftsministers vom 19. August 1938
betr. Auswertung der Anmeldung des Vermögens von Juden
und jüdisch Versippten. - III Jd 4499/38.-

Runderlass des Reichs- und Preussischen Ministers des
Innern zur Ausführung der dritten Durchführungsverordnung zum Reichsbürgergesetz bzgl. der Kennzeichnung
jüdischer Gewerbebetriebe vom 14. Juli 1938.

Erlass des Reichsfinanzministers vom 11. Juli 1938
bzgl. der Steuern für ausserordentliche Einkünfte.

Erlass des Reichsministers für Wissenschaft, Erziehung
und Volksbildung vom 1. Oktober 1938 bzgl. der Zulassung
von Gasthörern an den deutschen Hochschulen.

Erlass des Reichskommissars für die Wiedervereinigung
Österreichs mit dem Deutschen Reich vom 22. August 1938
bzgl. der Einrichtung einer Zentralstelle für jüdische
Auswanderung in Wien.

Erlass des Reichsministers des Innern für den Besuch
auswärtiger jüdischer Kurgäste in den Bädern und Kur-
orten.
Vom 15. Juni 1938 - le 7 XVI/38 5o12 e.

Verordnung zur Neuordnung des österreichischen Berufsbeamtentums vom 31. Mai 1938 (RGBl. I S. 6o7),

Anordnung des Reichsarbeitsministers vom 6. September
1938 bzgl. der Ausschliessung von jüdischen Verkaufsstellen von der Annahme der Reichsverbilligungsscheine
für Speisefette, der Bezugsscheine für Konsummargarine
und der kommunalen Wohlfahrtsscheine.
(RABl. Teil I, S. 313).

Erlass des Reichsministers des Innern bzgl. der Einquar-
tierung von Wehrmachtsangehörigen bei Juden vom 16. Juli
1938 - I RA. 197/38 2. Angabe
117.

Durchführung der Nürnberger Rassengesetze im Lande
Österreich.
RdErl. d. RMdI. vom 8. Juni 1938 - I d 198 II/38 - 5626.

Devisenrunderlass Nr. 57/38 DSt.-UeSt. vom 4. Juni 1938.

19

Mitteilung von Grundstücksgeschäften an die Finanz-
verwaltung.
AV. d. RIM vom 11. Mai 1938 (72o4 - IV. o^2 968).

Preussische Hauszinssteuerverordnung vom 3o. März 1938
(Gesetzsammlung, Seite 47).

Bekanntmachung des Reichsstatthalters in Österreich
über die Übertragung von Befugnissen nach den Vorschriften
über die Anmeldung des Vermögens von Juden und über die
Errichtung einer Vermögensverkehrsstelle im Ministerium
für Handel und Verkehr vom Mai 1938.

Waffengesetz vom 18. März 1938 (RGBl. I S 265)

Runderlass des Oberbürgermeisters der Stadt Berlin betr.
Krankenanstaltsversorgung der Juden in Berlin vom 3o.
März 1938 in Dienstblatt VII/38 Nr. 1o4.

Rundverfügung des Oberbürgermeisters der Reichshauptstadt
Berlin über die fachärztliche Versorgung jüdischer Wohlfahr-
fahrtspfleglinge, abgedruckt im Ärzteblatt für Berlin
und Kurmark, Heft 19, vom 7. Mai 1938.

Zweite Verordnung zur Durchführung des Grundsteuergesetzes
für den ersten Hauptveranlagungszeitraum (II. Gr.StDVO).
Vom 29. März 1938 (RGBl. I S.36o).

Gesetz zur Änderung des Gesetzes über das Schulgeld an
den öffentlichen höheren Schulen (Schulgeldgesetz) vom
8. Februar 1938 (Preuss. Gesetzsammlung, S. 15).

Anordnung des Reichsführers der Kassenärztlichen Vereinigung Deutschlands (KZVD.)vom 8. Januar 1938, bzgl. der
Beendigung der Tätigkeit jüdischer Zahnärzte für Mitglieder der Angestellten-Ersatzkassen und der Arbeiter-Ersatz-
kassen.

Drittes Gesetz zur Änderung der Vorschriften über die
Gebäudeentschuldungspflichtsteuerpflicht.
Vom 23. April 1938 (RGBl. I S.4o9).

Verordnung zur Durchführung des Gaststättengesetzes
vom 9. März 1938 (Pr.Ges. S.S. 25.)

Erlass des Reichswirtschaftsministers bzgl. der Frage
der Stellung der Juden in der Organisation der gewerblichen Wirtschaft vom Dezember 1937.

Erlass des Reichswirtschaftsministers vom 2o. Juni 1938
bzgl. der Nichtzulassung der Juden zum Börsenbesuch.

Erlass des Reichswirtschaftsministers bzgl. der Merkmale
Voraussetzungen des Vorliegens eines jüdischen Gewerbe-
betriebes. Vom März 1938.

Richtlinien des Oberkommandos der Wehrmacht bzgl. der
Miete bzw. Untermiete von Wehrmachtangehörigen bei Juden,
vom Juni 1938.

Erlass des österreichischen Ministeriums für Innere und
Kulturelle Angelegenheiten bzgl. der Behandlung jüdischer Schüler in Österreich vom Juni 1938.

Verordnung über die Einführung der Nürnberger Rassengesetze im Lande Österreich.
Vom 2o. Mai 1938 (RGBl. I S. 594).

Erlass des Reichspostministers vom 21. Juni 1938 bzgl.
Postwurfsendungen jüdischer Firmen (abgedruckt im Amts-
blatt des Reichspostministeriums 1938, S 367/68
vom 21. Juni 1938 - Nr. 7o.-)

Erlass des Reichs- und Preussischen Ministers für Er-
nährung und Landwirtschaft bzgl. ~~Zusatzes~~ eines Zusatzes
zur Trabrennordnung vom 3. Juni 1938 - III 2856.

Erlass des Reichsminsters des Innern vom 18. August 1938
(Verzeichnis der jüdischen Vornamen).

Anordnung des Beauftragten für den Vierjahresplan vom
26. April 1938 bzgl. der Veräusserung, Verpachtung und
Neueröffnung jüdischer Gewerbebetriebe.

~~Erlass des Reichsministers des Innern~~   **K325538**

Erlass des Reichsministers des Innern zum Reichsgesetz
über die Änderung und Ergänzung Familienrechtlicher Vorschriften bzgl. Ausschaltung der Juden vom Adoptionswe-
sen vom Oktober 1938.

Verordnung des Reicharbeitsministers über die Teilnahme
von Juden an der kassenärztlichen Versorgung vom 6. Oktober 1938.

Gesetz zur Ordnung der Krankenpflege vom 28. September
1938. (RGBl. I S. 13o9)

~~Ausführungsverordnung zum Gesetz zur Ordnung der Kranken-~~
~~pflege vom 28. September 1938.~~

Bekanntmachung des Beauftragten des Reichsärzteführers
im Stabe des Reichskommissars für das Land Österreich
bzgl. des Erlöschens der Bestallung jüdischer Ärzte und
Zahnärzte in Österreich.

Erste Verordnung über die berufsmässige Ausübung der Kran-
kenpflege und die Errichtung von Krankenpflegeschulen
(Krankenpflegeordnung) vom 28. September 1938 (RGBl. I
S. 131o)

Zweite Verordnung über die berufsmässige Ausübung der
Krankenpflege und die Errichtung von Krankenpflegeschu-
len (Ausführungsverordnung) vom 28. September 1938
(RGBl. I S. 1314)

                    AGR. Dr. Wetzel

OFFICE OF U.S. CHIEF OF COUNSEL
FOR THE PROSECUTION OF AXIS CRIMINALITY
Date 12 October 1945

STAFF EVIDENCE ANALYSIS

DESCRIPTION OF ATTACHED DOCUMENT (Under following headings).

Title and Nature: 1935 Reichgssetzblatt, part I, page 1146: The Reich Citizenship Law.

Date: 15 September 1935 . Copy   Language: German

LOCATION OF ORIGINAL (also WITNESS if applicable) as of ___12 October_____ 1945:

Unknown: Copy in OCC Files Nurnberg.

SOURCE OF ORIGINAL: Reichsgesetzblatt

PERSONS IMPLICATED: HITLER, Adolf; FRICK, Wilhelm

REFERENCES TO INDEX HEADINGS (Key to Par. nos. of Summary below):

Doc. 2

IDEOLOGY, NAZI: Racial Supremacy; PUBLICATIONS: Reichsgesetzblatt; REICH GOVERNMENT AGENCIES: Ministry of Interior.

22

NECESSARY PROCESSING TO PUT IN EVIDENTIARY FORM; LEADS: None

SUMMARY OF RELEVANT POINTS (with page references):

1. The Reich Citizenship Law as adopted unamiously by the Reichstag is promulgated in this document.

2. The prerequisite for citizenship is German or kindred blood.

3. The Law is signed by Hitler and Frick.

Analyst Landmann

1935 REICHSGESETBLATT, PART 1, PAGE 1146

The Reich Citizenship Law
of 15 Sept 1935

Reichsbuergergesetz
vom 15 Sept 1935

The Reichstag has adopted unanimously, the following law, which is herewith promulgated.

Article 1

1)A subject of the State is a person,who belongs to the protective union of the German Reich,and who, therefore,has particular obligations towards the Reich.

2)The status of the subject is acquired in accordance with the provisions of the Reich- and State Law of Citizenship.

Article 2

1)A citizen of the Reich is only that subject,who is of German or kindred blood and who,through his conduct,shows that he is both desirious and fit to serve faithfully the German people and Reich.

2)The right to citizenship is acquired by the granting of Reich citizenship papers.

3)Only the citizen of the Reich enjoys full political rights in accordance with the provisions of the Laws.

Article 3

The Reich Minister of the Interior in conjunction with the Deputy of the Fuehrer will issue the necessary legal and administrative decrees for the carrying out and supplementing of this law.

Nuernberg, 15 Sept 1935
at the Reichsparteitag fo Liberty

The Fuehrer and Reichs Chancellor
Adolf Hitler
The Reichs Minister of the Interior
Frick

- - - - - - - - - - - - -

CERTIFICATE OF TRANSLATION
OF DOCUMENT NO. 1416 & PS

27 September 1945

I,FRED NIEBERGALL,2nd Lt.Inf.,0-1335567,hereby certify that I am thoroughly conversant with the English and German languages; and that the above is a true and correct translation of Document 1416-PS.

FRED NIEBERGALL
2nd Lt. Inf.
0-1335567

I

Source: Reichsgesetzblatt, Part I, No. 100, of 16 September 1935

Law for the Protection of German Blood
and German Honor
. of 15 September 1935

Thoroughly convinced by the knowledge that the purity of German blood is essential for the further existence of the German people and inturned by the inflexible will to safe-guard the German nation for the entire future. The Reichs Parliament (Reichstag) has resolved upon the following law unanimously which is promulgated herewith:

Section L

1.   Marriages between Jews and nationals of German or kindred blood are forbidden. Marriages concluded in defiance of this law are void, even if, for the purpose of evading this law, they are concluded abroad.

2.   Proceedings for annulment may be initiated only by the Public Prosecutor.

Section 2

Relations outside marriage between Jews and nationals of German or kindred blood are forbidden.

Section 3

Jews will not be permitted to employ female nationals of German or kindred blood in their household.

Section 4

1.   Jews are forbidden to hoist the Reichs and national flag and to present the colors of the Reich.

2.   On the other hand they are permitted to present the Jewish colors. The exercise of this authority is protected by the State.

Section 5

1.   Who acts contrary to the prohibition of section 1 will be punished with hard labor.

2.   The man who acts contrary to the prohibition of section 2 will be punished with imprisonment or with hard labor.

3.   Who acts contrary to the provisions of sections 3 or 4 will be punished with imprisonment up to a year and with a fine or with one of these penalties.

Section 6

The Reich Minister of the Interior in agreement with the Deputy of the ' Fuehrer and the Reich Minister of Justice will issue the legal and administrative regulations which are required for the implementation and supplementation of this law.

Section 7

The law will become effective on the day after the promulgation, section 3 however only on the 1 January 1936.

Nurnberg, the 15 September 1935 at the Reich Party Rally of freedom.

The Fuehrer and Reich Chancellor
     Adolf Hitler

Doc. 3

24

Page 2

The Reich Minister of Interior
    Frick

The Reich Minister of Justice
    Dr. Gurtner

The Deputy of the Fuehrer
    R. Hess

Reich Minister without portfolio

CERTIFICATE OF TRANSLATION
OF DOCUMENT NO. 2000 PS

17 November 1945

I, MR. T.W. SCHONFELD, 51029, hereby certify that I am thoroughly conversant with the English and German languages; and that the above is a true and correct partial translation of Document No. 2000 PS.

T.W. SCHONFELD
51029

25

Doc. No. 1417-PS   Date .... 12 October 1945 ......

STAFF EVIDENCE ANALYSIS

DESCRIPTION OF ATTACHED DOCUMENT (Under following headings).

Title and Nature: 1935 Reichsesetzblatt, Part I, page 1933: First
Regulation to the Reich-citizenship Law of 14 November 1935 pertaining to
Jews.

Date: 14 November 1935 Original ( ) Copy (X) Language: German

LOCATION OF ORIGINAL: Reichgesetzblatt

PERSONS IMPLICATED: HITLER, Adolf; FRICK, Wilhelm; HESS, R udolf

REFERENCES TO INDEX HEADINGS (Key to Par. nos. of Summary below):

CIVIL LIBERTIES AND OTHER RIGHTS; IDEOLOGY, NAZI: Racial Supremacy;
JEWS PERSECUTION OF; REICH GOVERNMENT AGENCIES: Ministry of Interior;
PUBLICATIONS: Reichsgesetzblatt

Doc. 4

26

NECESSARY PROCESSING TO PUT IN EVIDENTIARY FORM: LEADS: None

SUMMARY OF RELEVANT POINTS (with page references):

1. The publication pertains to the determination "Jew" and stipulates that no Jew can be a Reich-citizen.

2. The publication deals with certain economic phases of Jewish
civil employees.

3. The document is signed by Hitler, Frick and Hess.

Analyst: Landmann   Doc. No. 1417-PS

Reichsgesetzblatt

Teil I

| 1935 | Ausgegeben zu Berlin, den 14. November 1935 | Nr. 125 |

Erste Verordnung zum Reichsbürgergesetz.

Vom 14. November 1935.

Auf Grund des § 3 des Reichsbürgergesetzes vom 15. September 1935 (Reichsgesetzbl. I S. 1146) wird folgendes verordnet:

§ 1

(1) Bis zum Erlaß weiterer Vorschriften über den Reichsbürgerbrief gelten vorläufig als Reichsbürger die Staatsangehörigen deutschen oder artverwandten Blutes, die beim Inkrafttreten des Reichsbürgergesetzes das Reichstagswahlrecht besessen haben, oder denen der Reichsminister des Innern im Einvernehmen mit dem Stellvertreter des Führers das vorläufige Reichsbürgerrecht verleiht.

(2) Der Reichsminister des Innern kann im Einvernehmen mit dem Stellvertreter des Führers das vorläufige Reichsbürgerrecht entziehen.

§ 2

(1) Die Vorschriften des § 1 gelten auch für die staatsangehörigen jüdischen Mischlinge.

(2) Jüdischer Mischling ist, wer von einem oder zwei der Rasse nach volljüdischen Großelternteilen abstammt, sofern er nicht nach § 5 Abs. 2 als Jude gilt. Als volljüdisch gilt ein Großelternteil ohne weiteres, wenn er der jüdischen Religionsgemeinschaft angehört hat.

§ 3

Nur der Reichsbürger kann als Träger der vollen politischen Rechte das Stimmrecht in politischen Angelegenheiten ausüben und ein öffentliches Amt bekleiden. Der Reichsminister des Innern oder die von ihm ermächtigte Stelle kann für die Übergangszeit Ausnahmen für die Zulassung zu öffentlichen Ämtern gestatten. Die Angelegenheiten der Religionsgesellschaften werden nicht berührt.

§ 4

(1) Ein Jude kann nicht Reichsbürger sein. Ihm steht ein Stimmrecht in politischen Angelegenheiten nicht zu; er kann ein öffentliches Amt nicht bekleiden.

(2) Jüdische Beamte treten mit Ablauf des 31. Dezember 1935 in den Ruhestand. Wenn diese Beamten im Weltkrieg an der Front für das Deutsche Reich oder für seine Verbündeten gekämpft haben, erhalten sie bis zur Erreichung der Altersgrenze als Ruhegehalt die vollen zuletzt bezogenen ruhegehaltsfähigen Dienstbezüge; sie steigen jedoch nicht in Dienstaltersstufen auf. Nach Erreichung der Altersgrenze wird ihr Ruhegehalt nach den letzten ruhegehaltsfähigen Dienstbezügen neu berechnet.

(3) Die Angelegenheiten der Religionsgesellschaften werden nicht berührt.

27

(4) Das Dienstverhältnis der Lehrer an öffentlichen jüdischen Schulen bleibt bis zur Neuregelung des jüdischen Schulwesens unberührt.

§ 5

(1) Jude ist, wer von mindestens drei der Rasse nach volljüdischen Großeltern abstammt. § 2 Abs. 2 Satz 2 findet Anwendung.

(2) Als Jude gilt auch der von zwei volljüdischen Großeltern abstammende staatsangehörige jüdische Mischling,

a) der beim Erlaß des Gesetzes der jüdischen Religionsgemeinschaft angehört hat oder danach in sie aufgenommen wird,

b) der beim Erlaß des Gesetzes mit einem Juden verheiratet war oder sich danach mit einem solchen verheiratet,

c) der aus einer Ehe mit einem Juden im Sinne des Absatzes 1 stammt, die nach dem Inkrafttreten des Gesetzes zum Schutze des deutschen Blutes und der deutschen Ehre vom 15. September 1935 (Reichsgesetzbl. I S. 1146) geschlossen ist,

d) der aus dem außerehelichen Verkehr mit einem Juden im Sinne des Absatzes 1 stammt und nach dem 31. Juli 1936 außerehelich geboren wird.

§ 6

(1) Soweit in Reichsgesetzen oder in Anordnungen der Nationalsozialistischen Deutschen Arbeiterpartei und ihrer Gliederungen Anforderungen an die Reinheit des Blutes gestellt werden, die über § 5 hinausgehen, bleiben sie unberührt.

(2) Sonstige Anforderungen an die Reinheit des Blutes, die über § 5 hinausgehen, dürfen nur mit Zustimmung des Reichsministers des Innern und des Stellvertreters des Führers gestellt werden. Soweit Anforderungen dieser Art bereits bestehen, fallen sie am 1. Januar 1936 weg, wenn sie nicht von dem Reichsminister des Innern im Einvernehmen mit dem Stellvertreter des Führers zugelassen werden. Der Antrag auf Zulassung ist bei dem Reichsminister des Innern zu stellen.

§ 7

Der Führer und Reichskanzler kann Befreiungen von den Vorschriften der Ausführungsverordnungen erteilen.

Berlin, den 14. November 1935.

Der Führer und Reichskanzler
Adolf Hitler

Der Reichsminister des Innern
Frick

Der Stellvertreter des Führers
R. Heß
Reichsminister ohne Geschäftsbereich

Erste Verordnung
zur Ausführung des Gesetzes zum Schutze des deutschen Blutes und der deutschen Ehre.
Vom 14. November 1935.

Auf Grund des § 6 des Gesetzes zum Schutze des deutschen Blutes und der deutschen Ehre vom 15. September 1935 (Reichsgesetzbl. I S. 1146) wird folgendes verordnet:

§ 1

(1) Staatsangehörige sind die deutschen Staatsangehörigen im Sinne des Reichsbürgergesetzes.

(2) Wer jüdischer Mischling ist, bestimmt § 2 Abs. 2 der Ersten Verordnung vom 14. November 1935 zum Reichsbürgergesetz (Reichsgesetzbl. I S. 1333).

(3) Wer Jude ist, bestimmt § 5 der gleichen Verordnung.

§ 2

Zu den nach § 1 des Gesetzes verbotenen Eheschließungen gehören auch die Eheschließungen zwischen Juden und staatsangehörigen jüdischen Mischlingen, die nur einen volljüdischen Großelternteil haben.

§ 3

(1) Staatsangehörige jüdische Mischlinge mit zwei volljüdischen Großeltern bedürfen zur Eheschließung mit Staatsangehörigen deutschen oder artverwandten Blutes oder mit staatsangehörigen jüdischen Mischlingen, die nur einen volljüdischen Großelternteil haben, der Genehmigung des Reichsministers des Innern und des Stellvertreters des Führers oder der von ihnen bestimmten Stelle.

(2) Bei der Entscheidung sind insbesondere zu berücksichtigen die körperlichen, seelischen und charakterlichen Eigenschaften des Antragstellers, die Dauer der Ansässigkeit seiner Familie in Deutschland, seine oder seines Vaters Teilnahme am Weltkrieg und seine sonstige Familiengeschichte.

(3) Der Antrag auf Genehmigung ist bei der höheren Verwaltungsbehörde zu stellen, in deren Bezirk der Antragsteller seinen Wohnsitz oder gewöhnlichen Aufenthalt hat.

(4) Das Verfahren regelt der Reichsminister des Innern im Einvernehmen mit dem Stellvertreter des Führers.

§ 4

Eine Ehe soll nicht geschlossen werden zwischen staatsangehörigen jüdischen Mischlingen, die nur einen volljüdischen Großelternteil haben.

§ 5

Die Ehehindernisse wegen jüdischen Bluteinschlages sind durch § 1 des Gesetzes und durch §§ 2 bis 4 dieser Verordnung erschöpfend geregelt.

§ 6

Eine Ehe soll ferner nicht geschlossen werden, wenn aus ihr eine die Reinerhaltung des deutschen Blutes gefährdende Nachkommenschaft zu erwarten ist.

§ 7

Vor der Eheschließung hat jeder Verlobte durch das Ehetauglichkeitszeugnis (§ 2 des Ehegesundheitsgesetzes vom 18. Oktober 1935 — Reichsgesetzbl. I S. 1246) nachzuweisen, daß kein Ehehindernis im Sinne des § 6 dieser Verordnung vorliegt. Wird das Ehetauglichkeitszeugnis versagt, so ist nur die Dienstaufsichtsbeschwerde zulässig.

§ 8

(1) Die Nichtigkeit einer entgegen dem § 1 des Gesetzes oder dem § 2 dieser Verordnung geschlossenen Ehe kann nur im Wege der Nichtigkeitsklage geltend gemacht werden.

(2) Für Ehen, die entgegen den §§ 3, 4 und 6 geschlossen worden sind, treten die Folgen des § 1 und des § 5 Abs. 1 des Gesetzes nicht ein.

§ 9

Besitzt einer der Verlobten eine fremde Staatsangehörigkeit, so ist vor einer Versagung des Aufgebotes wegen eines der im § 1 des Gesetzes oder in den §§ 2 bis 4 dieser Verordnung genannten Ehehindernisse sowie vor einer Versagung des Ehetauglichkeitszeugnisses in Fällen des § 6 die Entscheidung des Reichsministers des Innern einzuholen.

§ 10

Eine Ehe, die vor einer deutschen Konsularbehörde geschlossen ist, gilt als im Inlande geschlossen.

§ 11

Außerehelicher Verkehr im Sinne des § 2 des Gesetzes ist nur der Geschlechtsverkehr. Strafbar nach § 5 Abs. 2 des Gesetzes ist auch der außereheliche Verkehr zwischen Juden und staatsangehörigen jüdischen Mischlingen, die nur einen volljüdischen Großelternteil haben.

§ 12

(1) Ein Haushalt ist jüdisch (§ 3 des Gesetzes), wenn ein jüdischer Mann Haushaltungsvorstand ist oder der Hausgemeinschaft angehört.

(2) Im Haushalt beschäftigt ist, wer im Rahmen eines Arbeitsverhältnisses in die Hausgemeinschaft aufgenommen ist, oder wer mit alltäglichen Haushaltsarbeiten oder anderen alltäglichen, mit dem Haushalt in Verbindung stehenden Arbeiten beschäftigt ist.

29

(3) Weibliche Staatsangehörige deutschen oder artverwandten Blutes, die beim Erlaß des Gesetzes in einem jüdischen Haushalt beschäftigt waren, können in diesem Haushalt in ihrem bisherigen Arbeitsverhältnis bleiben, wenn sie bis zum 31. Dezember 1935 das 35. Lebensjahr vollendet haben.

(4) Fremde Staatsangehörige, die weder ihren Wohnsitz noch ihren dauernden Aufenthalt im Inlande haben, fallen nicht unter diese Vorschrift.

§ 13

Wer dem Verbot des § 3 des Gesetzes in Verbindung mit § 12 dieser Verordnung zuwiderhandelt, ist nach § 5 Abs. 3 des Gesetzes strafbar, auch wenn er nicht Jude ist.

§ 14

Für Verbrechen gegen § 5 Abs. 1 und 2 des Gesetzes ist im ersten Rechtszuge die große Strafkammer zuständig.

§ 15

Soweit die Vorschriften des Gesetzes und seiner Ausführungsverordnungen sich auf deutsche Staatsangehörige beziehen, sind sie auch auf Staatenlose anzuwenden, die ihren Wohnsitz oder gewöhnlichen Aufenthalt im Inlande haben. Staatenlose, die ihren Wohnsitz oder gewöhnlichen Aufenthalt im Auslande haben, fallen nur dann unter diese Vorschriften, wenn sie früher die deutsche Staatsangehörigkeit besessen haben.

§ 16

(1) Der Führer und Reichskanzler kann Befreiungen von den Vorschriften des Gesetzes und der Ausführungsverordnungen erteilen.

(2) Die Strafverfolgung eines fremden Staatsangehörigen bedarf der Zustimmung der Reichsminister der Justiz und des Innern.

§ 17

Die Verordnung tritt an dem auf die Verkündung folgenden Tage in Kraft. Den Zeitpunkt des Inkrafttretens des § 7 bestimmt der Reichsminister des Innern; bis zu diesem Zeitpunkt ist ein Ehetauglichkeitszeugnis nur in Zweifelsfällen vorzulegen.

Berlin, den 14. November 1935.

Der Führer und Reichskanzler
Adolf Hitler

Der Reichsminister des Innern
Frick

Der Stellvertreter des Führers
R. Heß
Reichsminister ohne Geschäftsbereich

Der Reichsminister der Justiz
Dr. Gürtner

Das Reichsgesetzblatt erscheint in zwei gesonderten Teilen — Teil I und Teil II —. Fortlaufender Bezug nur durch die Postanstalten. Bezugspreis vierteljährlich für Teil I = 1,75 *R.ℳ*, für Teil II = 2,10 *R.ℳ*. Einzelbezug jeder (auch jeder älteren) Nummer nur vom **Reichsverlagsamt**, Berlin NW 40, Scharnhorststraße Nr. 4 (Fernsprecher: D 2 Weidendamm 9265 — Postscheckkonto: Berlin 96200). Einzelnummern werden nach dem Umfang berechnet. Preis für den achtseitigen Bogen 15 *Rpf*, aus abgelaufenen Jahrgängen 10 *Rpf*, ausschließlich der Postdrucksachengebühr. Bei größeren Bestellungen 10 bis 60 v. H. Preisermäßigung. Herausgegeben vom Reichsministerium des Innern. — Gedruckt in der Reichsdruckerei, Berlin.

1935 REICHSGESETZBLATT, PART 1, PAGE 1333

First Regulation to the Reichs Citizenship Law
of 14 Nov. 1935

Erste Verordnung zum Reichsbürgergesetz
vom 14, Nov. 1935

On the basis of Article 3, Reichs Citizenship Law, of 15 Sept. 1935 (R.G.Bl I, page 1146) the following is ordered:

Article 1

(1) Until further issue of regulations regarding citizenship papers, all subjects of German or kindred blood, who possessed the right to vote in the Reichstag elections, at the time the Citizenship Law came into effect, shall, for the time being, possess the rights of Reich citizens. The same shall be true of those whom the Reich Minister of the Interior, in conjunction with the Deputy of the Fuehrer, has given the preliminary citizenship.

(2) The Reich Minister of the Interior, in conjunction with the Deputy of the Fuehrer, can withdraw the preliminary citizenship.

Article 2

(1) The regulations in Article 1 are also valid for Reichs subjects of mixed, Jewish blood.

(2) An individual of mixed Jewish blood, is one who descended from one or two grandparents who were racially full Jews, insofar as does not count as a Jew according to Article 5, paragraph 2. One grandparent shall be considered as full-blooded Jew if he or she belonged to the Jewish religious community.

Article 3

Only the Reich citizen, as bearer of full political rights, exercises the right to vote in political affairs, and can hold a public office. The Reich Minister of the Interior, or any agency empowered by him, can make exceptions during the transition period, with regard to occupying public offices. The affairs of religious organizations will not be touched upon.

Article 4

(1) A Jew cannot be a citizen of the Reich. He has no right to vote in political affairs; he cannot occupy a public office.

(2) Jewish officials will retire as of 31 December 1935. If these officials served at the front in the World War, either for Germany or her allies, they will receive in full, until they reach the age limit, the pension to which they were entitled according to last received wages; they will, however, not advance in seniority. After reaching the age limit, their pension will be calculated anew, according to the last received salary, on the basis of which their pension was computed.

(3) The affairs of religious organizations will not be touched upon.

(4) The conditions of service of teachers in Jewish public schools remain unchanged, until new regulations of the Jewish school systems are issued.

Article 5

(1) A Jew is anyone who descended from at least three grandparents who were racially full Jews. Article 2, par. 2, second sentence will apply.

(2) A Jew is also one who descended from two full Jewish parents, if:

31

(a) he belonged to the Jewish religious community at the time
this law was issued, or who joined the community later.
(b) he was married to a Jewish person, at the time the law was
issued, or married one subsequently.
(c) he is the offspring from a marriage with a Jew, in the sense
of Section 1, which was contracted after the Law for the
protection of German blood and German honor became effective
(RGBl. I, page 1146 of 15 Sept 1935).
(d) he is the offspring of an extramarital relationship, with a
Jew, according to Section 1, and will be born out of wedlock
after July 31, 1936.

Article 6

(1) As far as demands are concerned for the pureness of blood as
laid down in Reichs law or in orders of the N.S.D.A.P. and its echelons - not
covered in Article 5 - they will not be touched upon.

(2) Any other demands on pureness of blood, not covered in Article 5,
can only be made with permission from the Reich Minister of the Interior and
the Deputy of the Fuehrer. If any such demands have been made, they will be
void as of 1 Jan 1936, if they have not been requested from the Reich Minister
of the Interior in agreement with the Deputy of the Fuehrer. These requests
must be made from the Reich Minister of the Interior.

Article 7

The Fuehrer and Reichs Chancellor can grant exemptions from the
regulations laid down in the law.

Berlin, 14 November 1935

The Fuehrer and Reichs Chancellor
Adolf Hitler
The Reich Minister of the Interior
Frick
The Deputy of the Fuehrer
R. Hess
- Reich Minister without Portfolio -

- - - - - -

CERTIFICATE OF TRANSLATION
OF DOCUMENT NO 1417-PS

28 September 1945

I, FRED NIEBERGALL, 2nd Lt Inf, O-1335567, hereby certify that I am
thoroughly conversant with the English and German languages; and that the
above is a true and correct translation of Document 1417-PS.

FRED NIEBERGALL
2nd Lt Inf
O-1335567

Sch./Ha.   6

Lageberioht

der Abteilung II 112 .

Doc. 5

33

April - Mai 1936.

Berlin,den 25.Juni 1936.

Gliederung.

34

35

Die innerpolitische Lage der Judenheit im Reich hat eine wesentliche Änderung während der Berichtszeit kaum erfahren. Lediglich die Ereignisse in Palästina haben eine leichte Unruhe in beiden Lagern hervorgerufen, die von den Assimilanten allgemein als antipalästinensische Propaganda tatkräftig ausgenutzt wird. Die Zionisten hingegen versuchen durch führende Anhänger mit einer wesentlich erhöhten Werbung für die Palästinaauswanderung an die jüdische Öffentlichkeit zu treten, die unter dem Motto "Nun erst recht" die derzeitigen Unruhen in "Erez Israel" zu bagatellisieren beabsichtigt.

Obwohl diese Agitation im allgemeinen ihr gesetztes Ziel nicht verfehlt, werden aus einigen Teilen des Reiches Rückwanderungsbestrebungen und teilweise Einschränkungen der Palästinaauswanderung gemeldet.

Referat II 112 1 (Assimilanten).

36

Politische Vereinigungen:

Der "Centralverein der Juden in Deutschland" führt seit langer Zeit grösstenteils nur noch ein Scheindasein. Mitgliederversammlungen werden im allgemeinen nicht mehr gemeldet. Nur in München wird neuerdings versucht, sich wieder etwas bemerkbar zu machen. Es wurden dort in letzter Zeit auffallend häufig in Strassenbahnen Bücherverzeichnisse und Reklameschriften des C.V. gefunden. Die Münchener Ortsgruppe versucht in letzter Zeit ihren Mitgliedern Freifahrten nach Palästina zu ermöglichen, damit sich diese von der Unmöglichkeit der zionistischen Idee durch Tatsachen überzeugen sollen.

Wesentlich anders arbeitet der "Reichsbund jüdischer Frontsoldaten". Auch er macht zweifellos keinen Hehl aus seiner antizionistischen Einstellung, versucht aber darüber hinaus seine Existenzberechtigung auf anderer Basis zu beweisen. Das immer wieder in den Vordergrundschieben der ehemaligen Fronttätigkeit seiner

Mitglieder ist hinreichend bekannt. Einige Ortsgruppen versuchen durch Beziehungen zu arischen Offiziersverbänden die Prinzipien des RjF zu festigen und auszubauen. In München sind z.B. derartige Bestrebungen beobachtet worden. In Oppeln in Oberschlesien hatte die Ortsgruppe des RjF unter Berufung auf das Minderheitenabkommen um eine geschlossene Teilnahme ihrer Mitglieder an einer Gedenkfeier der Wehrmacht gebeten. Es wurde versucht, durch Vorlage eines Gedenkbuches für die gefallenen Juden die Berechtigung dafür nachzuweisen. Der Standort der Wehrmacht lehnte die Beteiligung ab.

Sein Hauptbetätigungsfeld findet der RjF z.Zt. in der Propagierung und Vorbereitung der Auswanderung in ausserpalästinensische Länder, vorwiegend nach Übersee. Er unterhält dabei neuerdings enge Beziehungen zur "JCA - Jewish Colonisation Association" und erhofft sich von ihr wirksame Durchführung seiner Pläne. In letzter Zeit besteht ebenso ein gutes Einvernehmen der Bundesführung mit der englisch-jüdischen Frontkämpferlegion. Man beabsichtigt dadurch Möglichkeiten für eine Auswanderung nach englischen Kolonien zu bekommen. Zur Vorbereitung der Auswanderung beabsichtigt die "Reichsvertretung der Juden in Deutschland" in Gross-Bressen bei Breslau ein Lehrgut einzurichten, das vorwiegend von RjF-Anhängern benutzt werden soll.

In seiner jüdischen Propagandamethodik wenden sich die Anhänger auch gegen den C.V. Der RjF allein sei berufen, die Interessen des Judentums in Deutschland zu vertreten.

Immer wieder bedauert wird in RjF-Kreisen die Ausschaltung der Juden vom Wehrdienst. Die jüdische Jugend müsste sich mehr denn je sportlich betätigen, um dafür einen Ausgleich zu schaffen. -

Es wird abzuwarten sein, wieweit dem RjF diese überall festzustellende Isolierung zugute kommt.

Einzelne Ortsgruppen des "Reichsverbandes nichtarischer Christen" erfreuen sich nicht nur in der nichtarischen Christenheit sondern auch in führenden Kreisen der Geistlichkeit grosser Beliebtheit. In Düsseldorf nahm an einer Gründungsversammlung der evangelische Pastor F l a t o w aus Köln teil. Weitere Gründungsversammlungen fanden statt in Köln, Aachen und Essen. Die Ortsgruppe Hannover des Reichsverbandes beabsichtigt sich in einen Landesverband zu vergrössern. Wie in Westdeutschland, so ist auch

37

in München der nichtarische Christenbund sehr aktiv. Es sind immer
wieder Bestrebungen wahrzunehmen, die darauf abgestellt sind, über
diesen Verband und vielleicht mit Hilfe irgendwelcher Verwand-
schaftsverhältnisse einen Einfluss in Partei und Staat zu bekommen.
Wieweit das bisher gelungen ist, konnte nicht festgestellt werden.

Der "Verband nationaldeutscher Juden" tritt nach seiner
Auflösung nicht mehr in Erscheinung. Seine Mitglieder sind grösstenteils in das Lager des RjF. übergegangen; einige besitzen heute
die Mitgliedschaft im CV.

Religiöse Vereinigungen:

Eine aktive religiöse Betätigung in Assimilantenkreisen
ist nicht festzustellen. Über den "Verein für das rel.-lib. Judentum" liegen keinerlei Meldungen vor.

Jugendvereinigungen:

Die assimilatorischen Jugendvereine haben vereinzelt
Mitgliederabgänge zu verzeichnen. Im allgemeinen ist die Betätigung
gleichmässig. Heimabende und kleinere interne Veranstaltungen fül-
len das Programm des "Ring - Bund jüd. Jugend" (früher BdjJ.). In
Berlin gab das Verhalten eines Zuges des "Ring" Veranlassung, von
staatspolizeilicher Seite gegen ihn einzuschreiten. Etwa 5o Mitglieder waren getrennt nach einem gleichen Ziel marschiert und
hatten sich dort einheitlich uniformiert. Die Staatspolizei Berlin
hat daraufhin dem Berliner "Ring" jegliche Betätigung für die Dauer eines Monats untersagt.

Sportvereinigungen:

Auf dem Gebiete des Sports ist der RjF. mit seinen Sport-
bünden führend. Die Betätigung ist im allgemeinen überall sehr re-
ge. Es ist immer wieder festzustellen, dass der RjF. versucht, auch
auf den entlegensten Gebieten des Sports vorherrschend zu sein. So
werden jetzt vielfach Keglervereinigungen ins Leben gerufen. (Hannover und Berlin). In Frankfurt/M. ist ein Mitglied des RjF. an den
"Reichsverband Deutscher Sportfischer" herangetreten und hat um
Erlaubnis nachgesucht, einen nichtarischen Anglerclub gründen zu
dürfen. Wegen Mangel an Beteiligung ist eine offizielle Gründung
nicht erfolgt.

-4-

Berufsumschichtung:

        Über assimilatorische Berufsumschulungsorganisationen
liegen bisher wenig Meldungen vor. Der vom "Ring - BjJ." ins Leben gerufene "Kreis deutsch-jüdischer Selbsthilfe Land und Hand-
werk" tritt nicht mehr in Erscheinung . Auch die für die Südameri-
kaumschulung vom "Ring" im Einvernehmen mit dem RjF. aufgezogene
Auswandererschule arbeitet bisher noch nicht. Die "Reichsvertretung der Juden in Deutschland' schuf letzthin mehrere Auswanderungs-
möglichkeiten. Sie hat in Rüdnitz im Kreise Oberbarnim bei Berlin
ein Umschulungslager eingerichtet und unterhält in Berlin-Nieder-
schönhausen eine Tagesschule für Berufslehre.

Frauenvereinigungen:

        Die ass. Frauenvereine veranstalten Haushaltungskurse
für junge Jüdinnen, die an die Stelle der bisherigen arischen Haus-
angestellten treten sollen, die auf Grund des Nürnberger Gesetzes
aus jüdischen Haushalten scheiden mussten. Ausserdem ist vereinzelt beabsichtigt, besondere Kurse für junge Mädchen einzurichten,
um ihnen praktischen Unterricht über Sitten und Gebräuche in den
Auswanderungsländern zu erteilen.

        Mit besonderen Veranstaltungen treten die Frauenvereine
nicht hervor. Neben kleineren Kränzchen nehmen ihre Mitglieder an
gemeinsamen "Familienveranstaltungen" der grossen Organisationen,
insbesondere des RjF., teil.

39

        Referat II 112 2 (Religiöse und Mittelgruppen). ·
        ==

Politische Vereinigungen:

        Die Betätigung des U.O.B.B. ist überall sehr regelmässig.
Die Mitglieder kommen nach wie vor zu ihren Logenabenden zusammen.
Eine rituelle Arbeit findet im allgemeinen nicht mehr statt. Den
Hauptinhalt eines Logenabends bilden Vorträge über politische Er-
eignisse, denen sich zumeist ein gemütlicher Teil anschliesst.

        Von etwa 1oo Logen, die 1933 noch bestanden, sind heute
34 suspendiert. Ausser den 66 noch arbeitenden bestehen ungefähr

25 Schwesternvereinigungen auf das gesamte Reichsgebiet verteilt.

Von der Grossloge des U.O.B.B. war beabsichtigt, jüdische Kinder durch Vermittlung ausländischer Grosslogen in die Tschechoslowakei und nach Holland zu verschicken. Das Geheime Staatspolizeiamt hat eine solche Verschickung ins Ausland nur für Kinder im Alter von 6-10 Jahren gestattet.

Die Arbeit des "Verband polnischer Juden" erforderte in letzter Zeit erhöhte Aufmerksamkeit. Seine Betätigung beschränkte sich dabei auf bestimmte Städte. In Dresden fand eine grössere Veranstaltung statt, die als Gedenkfeier zu Ehren des Marschalls Pilsudski geschickt getarnt war. Die versandten Einladungskarten waren mit polnischem und übersetztem deutschen Text versehen. Der deutsche Absender lautete "Verein polnischer Staatsbürger e.V. Dresden", während der polnische Text übersetzt hiess "Verein polnischer Staatsbürger jüdischen Glaubens e.V. Dresden". Der polnische Vizekonsul hielt eine kurze Gedenkrede auf Pilsudki, die den Eindruck erweckte, als sei sie nur zur Tarnung angesetzt.

Die "Agudas Jisroel" tritt wenig in Erscheinung. Ihre Betätigung ist sehr zurückhaltend. Die Unruhen in Palästina haben dazu wesentlich beigetragen. Sahen die Agudas-Anhänger schon allein in der Ansiedlung von Zionisten in Palästina eine Profanierung des gelobten und geheiligten Landes, so sind sie durch die derzeitigen blutigen Kämpfe einfach sprachlos und erschüttert. Die Sammeltätigkeit für den "Keren Hajischuw" hat ganz aufgehört.

Ihre Hauptstützpunkte hat die Agudas in Hamburg, Köln, Berlin, München und Karlsruhe. In anderen Orten ist sie nur wenig vertreten.

Religiöse Vereinigungen (Gemeinden):

In den jüdischen Gemeinden bestehen nach wie vor Meinungsverschiedenheiten. Zionisten fordern das sogenannte Fifty-Fifty-Prinzip, das ihnen die Hälfte der Sitze in den Gemeindevertretungen zusichert. Dieses Prinzip ist noch nicht überall durchgeführt. In den Synagogengemeinden Breslau's wurden jetzt zum ersten Male zionistische Vertreter in die Ausschüsse gewählt.

Während in einigen Teilen des Reiches die Gemeinden über ausreichende Geldmittel zu verfügen scheinen (Grossgemeinde Breslau), sodass jüdischen Sportvereienen für ihre Zwecke finanzielle

-6-

Unterstützungen gewährt werden konnten, sind andere Gemeinden am
Ende ihrer finanziellen Leistungsfähigkeit.

In Bremen musste das Gemeindeblatt der israelitischen
Gemeinde sein Erscheinen wegen Mangel an Auflage einstellen.

Jugendvereinigungen:

Über neutrale Jugendvereine, die "Agudas-Jugend" und den
"Jüdisch-orthodoxen Jugendbund Esra" liegen keine besonderen Meldungen vor.

Die Arbeit der Jugendgemeinschaften der Gemeinden erstreckt sich hauptsächlich auf die einfache Unterhaltung seiner
jungen Mitglieder. Eine besondere Betätigung auf anderen Gebieten
konnte nicht festgestellt werden.

Berufsvereinigungen:

Unter den Berufsvereinen nimmt im jüdischen Leben der
"Centralverband jüdischer Handwerker Deutschlands" eine besondere
Stellung ein. Seine Ortsgruppen sind allgemein sehr aktiv.

Die Ortsgruppe Hannover des Verbandes hat beschlossen,
im Juni Berufswettkämpfe im Bezirk Hannover durchzuführen und die
besten Arbeiten in einer Ausstellung der jüdischen Öffentlichkeit
zu zeigen.

Die Breslauer Ortsgruppe feierte am 9.5.1936 ihr fünf-
undzwanzigjähriges Bestehen. In der Festansprache wurde ausdrücklich davor gewarnt, jüdische Kinder in zu starkem Ausmass den Hand-
werksberuf erlernen zu lassen.

Caritative Vereinigungen:

Die "Jüdische Winterhilfe" hat in einigen Bezirken grosse Erfolge zu verzeichnen gehabt. Eine Reichsbilanz liegt hier
z.Zt. noch nicht vor, wird aber in nächster Zeit zusammengestellt.
Die einzelnen Gemeinden haben grösstenteils für ihren Bereich bereits Bilanzen aufgestellt. Solche sind übersandt aus dem Gebiet
des Oberabschnitts Nordwest. Auch in anderen O.A. wird sich die
Beschaffung, nach Möglichkeit unter restloser Erfassung des Be-
reiches, empfehlen.

41

Schulwerk:

Durch gesetzliche Anordnung müssen jüdische Kinder die jüdischen Volksschulen besuchen. Die massgeblichen jüdischen Instanzen sahen darin eine Veranlassung, das jüdische Schulwesen weiterhin auszubauen. Aus einigen Orten werden Gründungen von jüdischen Privatschulen mit der Gelegenheit zur Erreichung der Reife für Obersekunda gemeldet. Grosser Wert wird überall auf das Erlernen der hebräischen Sprache gelegt. Neuhebräisch ist vielfach als Pflichtfach eingeführt.

Kulturelle Vereinigungen:

Das Wirken der Kulturbünde im "Reichsverband jüdischer Kulturbünde" ist im Reichsgebiet wenig einheitlich. Während die Spitze des Reichsverbandes durch das Präsidieren des Führers der "Staatszionistischen Vereinigung", Georg Kareski, staatszionistisch orientiert ist, macht sich in den einzelnen Bünden und Ortsgruppen immer wieder der vorwiegend assimilatorische Einfluss bemerkbar, so z.B. in Breslau.

Politische Hilfsorganisationen:

Der "Hilfsverein der Juden in Deutschland" tritt propagandistisch kaum noch in Erscheinung. Dagegen betreibt er mit erhöhter Intensität die Auswanderungsvermittlung seiner Mitglieder. Nur vereinzelt sind Veranstaltungen gemeldet, in denen für die Auswanderung nach Übersee geworben wird.

Dem "Zentralausschuss der deutschen Juden für Hilfe und Aufbau" ist die gesamte Betreuung der jüdischen Wohlfahrt übertragen. Er untersteht direkt der Aufsicht der Reichsvertretung. In seinen Händen lag die Durchführung der jüdischen Winterhilfe.

In Stuttgart trat der Zentralausschuss an die jüdischen Gemeindemitglieder mit einem Aufruf, in dem er seine Ziele und Aufgaben, Hilfe für die notleidenden Glaubensgenossen und Unterstützung der heranwachsenden Jugend beim Aufbau neuer Existenzen, hervorhebt und zum Erwerb einer Spendenkarte auffordert. Im Rahmen dieser Sammlung wurden im Mai zunächst von der jüdischen Schuljugend alle diejenigen Juden aufgesucht, die bereits schon zum JWH gespendet hatten.

Über Mitglieder des "Ort" liegen von den O.A. keine Mel-

dungen vor. In den einzelnen Orten des Reiches bestehen keine orga-
nisatorischen Zusammenfassungen. Sämtliche Mitglieder, insgesamt
etwa 4oo, gehören direkt der "Ort-Gesellschaft, Abteilung Deutschland e.V."in Berlin an.

In nächster Zeit erfolgt besonderer Bericht über den"Ort"
und Anweisung über seine Bearbeitung.

Referat II 112 3 (Zionisten).

Die letzten Ereignisse in Palästina sind nicht achtlos
an der zionistisch eingestellten Judenheit vorbeigegangen. Es wurde schon eingangs erwähnt, dass der Grossteil der Zionisten in
Deutschland mit aller Energie und Verbissenheit versucht, auf je-
den Fall das grosse Ziel "Erez Israel" auch weiterhin im Auge zu
behalten und auch weiterhin für eine möglichst starke Abwanderung
Sorge zu tragen.

Die Mandatsmacht England hat die jüdische Einwanderungs-
quote für Palästina erhöht, sodass auch dem Palästinaamt der Jewish Agency in Zukunft mehr Zertifikate für deutsche Zionisten zur
Verfügung gestellt werden dürften.

Es entstehen,vom Standpunkt des Gegners gesehen, im Ge-
samtzionismus in Deutschland ungewollt und unbewusst 3 Lager: Das
kleinste, das sich voller Angst, seinen Anhängern könnte es im Falle einer Auswanderung genau so ergehen wie Hunderten von "Chawerim"
in diesen Wochen, versucht zurückzuziehen und die Auswanderung ein-
zuschränken; das zweite und grösste, das bedenkenlos einfach die
blutigen Unruhen zu vertuschen versucht, sie vielleicht zugibt, die
eigentlichen Hintergründe aber nicht wahr haben will; das dritte,
dessen Anhänger mit ausgeprägtem Fanatismus immer wieder agitieren
und für eine Verteidigung Palästinas, erforderlichenfalls mit Waf-
fengewalt,eintreten.

Das erste Lager ist, wie schon gesagt, verschwindend klein
und bedeutungslos. Rückwanderungen wurden vereinzelt in Pommern
festgestellt.

Als den Propagandisten der zweiten Richtung hörig sind
die Konjunkturzionisten anzusehen, die weder aus innerer Überzeu-

43

gung noch aus besonderem Mut nationaljüdisch denken oder fühlen,
die nur Zionisten sind, weil sie irgendwie den Anschluss an ihre
Rassegenossen behalten wollen. Ihnen wird es ganz gleichgültig
sein, ob in Palästina wieder einmal einige Juden mehr daran glauben müssen; sie selbst werden Palästina nie sehen.

Die dritte Gruppe rekrutiert sich aus den langjährigen
alten Zionisten und in erhöhtem Masse den Staatszionisten.

Ein vereinendes Band verbindet jedoch alle Altzionisten
in Deutschland: Die Hoffnung auf die Mandatsmacht England. In vie-
len Reden ihrer führenden Männer kommt das immer wieder zum Aus-
druck.

Die Staatszionisten sind dabei ziemlich zurückhaltend.
Obwohl sie immer für jüdische Selbstverteidigung in Palästina of-
fen eintreten, haben sie gegenüber England als Mandatsmacht wenig
Sympathien. Sie würden es vorziehen, wenn Italien das Mandat über
Palästina übernehmen würde.

Alte Zionisten.

Politische Vereinigungen:

Die "ZVfD" und ihre Ortsgruppen als Hauptträger der zionistischen Idee in Deutschland sind nach wie vor sehr aktiv. Die
häufig abgehaltenen Veranstaltungen bewegen sich in dem üblichen
Rahmen.

In Gleiwitz fand am 26.4.1936 eine zionistische Gruppen-
verbandstagung für die oberschlesischen Gruppen statt. Im Mittelpunkt der Tagung stand eine Arbeitsgemeinschaft über nationale und
Mittelstandskolonisation in Palästina.

Interessant sind die Ausführungen des Rabbiner Dr.Grün-
wald,Mannheim, auf einer Tagung des Gruppenverbandes Baden, Würt-
temberg, Pfalz über "Überseewanderung und zionistische Planung".
Grünwald erklärte grundsätzlich, dass eine Überseewanderung vom
Zionismus nicht abgelehnt werde, sofern es möglich ist, die Auswan-
derer vor ihrem Weggang innerlich so zu festigen, dass sie dem
Zionismus nicht verloren gehen.

Jugend- und Umschichtungsvereinigungen:

Naturgemäss sind es gerade die Jugendvereine, die mit

allen Mitteln versuchen, auch praktische Zionisten zu sein. Durch hebräischen Unterricht in ihren Mitgliederkreisen wird überall die Voraussetzung zur Auswanderung geschaffen.

Auf dem jüdischen Lehrgut "Winkel" bei Spreenhagen bei Berlin fand vom 15.4. bis 1.5.1936 eine Führertagung des "Makkabi Hazair" statt. Es nahmen 62 Mitglieder teil.

Die Arbeit des "Hechaluz" bot im allgemeinen wenig Neues.

Sportvereinigungen:

Als Gegengewicht zum Sportbund des RJF versucht der "Makkabi" alle zionistischen Sportler zu erfassen. Sportliche Wettkämpfe stehen im Mittelpunkt des Vereinslebens.

Palästinawerk:

Ein Ende Mai erschienener Aufruf des "Keren Hajessod", in dem zur Entrichtung eines Sonderbeitrages aufgefordert wurde, wurde von der ZVfD tatkräftig unterstützt.

Am 17.5.1936 ist eine Werbeaktion des "Keren Kajemeth Lejisroel (KKL)" abgeschlossen worden, über deren Ergebnis noch nichts bekannt ist.

Staatszionisten:

Über die Betätigung von staatszionistischen Ortsgruppen im Reich ist nichts besonderes bekannt geworden. Aus Zwickau i.Sa. wird gemeldet, dass sich die dortige staatszionistische Ortsgruppe wegen Mangel an Mitgliedern aufgelöst hat.

Der "Brith Hechajal" ist durch staatliche Anordnung aufgelöst worden. Obwohl seine Mitgliederzahl von jeher ziemlich gering war, durfte seine Bedeutung als staatszionistische Wehrorganisation nicht unterschätzt werden.

Am aktivsten sind die Gruppen des staatszionistischen Jugendbundes "Jüdisch-nationale Jugend Herzlia (Betar)". In Berlin zählt er etwa 5oo Mitglieder beiderlei Geschlechts. Die Erziehung bei internen Veranstaltung ist bewusst soldatisch. Mit staatlicher Genehmigung tragen die Mitglieder dunkelbraune Hemden bezw. Blusen mit blauem Kragen, Ärmelaufschlägen und Achselklappen. Es konnte festgestellt werden, dass Berliner Heime des "Betar" öffentlich die blau-weisse Zionistenfahne zu Ehren der in Palästina gefallenen

45

Juden auf Halbmast setzten. Nach den Nürnberger Gesetzen stehen
jüdische Fahnen unter staatlichem Schutz.

In Danzig ist eine Ortsgruppe der "Neuen zionistischen
Organisation" gegründet worden, die als solche der staatszionistischen Vereinigung in Deutschland nicht angehört.

Allgemeine jüdische Betätigung.
===

Jüdische Organisationen untereinander:

Das Verhältnis der jüdischen Organisationen untereinander
ist allgemein kein gutes. Nur vereinzelt treten Einigungsbestre-
bungen offen auf, in Halle a.S. haben sich sämtliche jüdischen
Jugendvereine zu einem "Ortsring jüdischer Jugendvereine" zusammen-
geschlossen. Grösstenteils werden solche Bestrebungen von zionisti-
scher Seite sabotiert. In Dortmund ist den zionistischen Turnern
von der ZOG nahegelegt worden, unter allen Umständen eine gemein-
same Betätigung mit dem RjF zu unterlassen.

In Rostock versuchen führende Köpfe assimilatorischer
Verbände durch besondere Intelligenz die Zionisten zu übertrumpfen.

Verhältnis zu Staatsstellen:

Die Einstellung jüdischer Organisationen ist sehr zurückhaltend. Nur der RjF glaubt, eine Bevorzugung erfahren zu müssen.
Er beruft sich auf die ihm von der NSKOV übertragene Aufgabe der
Betreuung jüdischer Kriegsopfer. Von den Staatspolizeistellen wird
dieses Ansinnen energisch zurückgewiesen.

Die Einstellung von Behörden Juden gegenüber wird den
nationalsozialistischen Anforderungen nicht immer voll gerecht. So
ist in Wismar bei der Stadtverwaltung noch immer ein Volljude beschäftigt, der nach den Ausführungsbestimmungen zu den Nürnberger
Gesetzen vom November 1935 zum 31.12.1935 hätte pensioniert werden
müssen.

Der Reichsärzteführer hat vor einiger Zeit über jüdische
Ärzte eine Anordnung erlassen. Die Begriffsbestimmung "Jude" wurde
für das Ärztewesen der Festlegung in den Nürnberger Gesetzen ange-
glichen. Vertretungen von Ärzten dürfen in Zukunft nur durch Gleich-
rassige erfolgen. Es geht danach nicht mehr an, dass sich ein ari-

scher Arzt während seiner Abwesenheit von einem Juden vertreten
lässt.

Verhältnis zu Partei und Nebenorganisationen:

Eine Ortsgruppe des Reichsluftschutzbundes im Westen
des Reiches hat Anfang Mai einen Gasschutzkursus durchgeführt, an
dem 30 männliche und 30 weibliche Juden beteiligt waren. Die Anordnung zu dieser Schulung soll die Gauführung des RLB in Hannover ge-
geben haben.

Verhältnis zur Wehrmacht:

Noch immer wieder besagen Meldungen, dass einzelne Trup-
penteile ihren Bedarf bei jüdischen Händlern decken. In Ostpreussen
befindet sich noch heute fast der gesamte Pferdehandel in jüdischen
Händen. So sei die Wehrmacht gezwungen, ihre Remonten bei Juden
einzukaufen.

Auch aus München werden Lieferungen von Juden an Heeres-
verpflegungsämter gemeldet.

Verhältnis zur Wirtschaft:

Auf die deutsche Wirtschaft hat der Jude nach wie vor
einen massgeblichen Einfluss. Ein Eingehen auf Einzeldinge würde
hier zu weit führen.

Der Verkaufsdirektor Dienemann der jüdischen Firma
Scherk G.m.b.H., Berlin, betreibt seine Werbung neuerdings in Hannover mit dem Hinweis, selbst Frauen führender deutscher Staats-
männer decken ihren Bedarf bei Scherk in Berlin.

Immer wieder muss festgestellt werden, dass die Bekäm-
pfung jüdischer Warenhäuser an dem Verhalten der Volksgenossen
selbst scheitert. Parteigenossen und Nichtparteigenossen scheuen
sich nicht, weiterhin, teilweise sogar in Uniform, ihre Einkäufe
bei Juden zu tätigen.

Es wurde berichtet, dass der Verkauf kleinerer jüdischer
Geschäfte an Nichtjuden, besonders in Provinzstädten, weiterhin
anhält.

Verhältnis zur Justiz:

Mit allen Mitteln beabsichtigen Juden immer wieder, die

47

Nürnberger Gesetze zu umgehen. Aus Holland, Österreich und der Tschechoslowakei werden Angestellte für jüdische Haushalte vermittelt. In Chemnitz wurde jedoch die Feststellung gemacht, dass es tschechische Staatsangehörige ablehnten, bei Juden in Dienste zu treten. Aus München wird berichtet, dass Hausangestellte entlassen werden und als "Betriebsangestellte" im gleichen Haushalt bezw. Betrieb wieder Anstellung finden.

Die Staatspolizeistelle in Breslau vermittelt jüdischen Haushalten Angestellte auf folgende Art:
Fünf jüdische Breslauer Dirnen sind nach Absolvierung eines Kursus in einem Zwangslager der jüdischen Arbeitsfürsorge zur Vermittlung als Hausmädchen in jüdischen Haushalten überwiesen worden. Zwei von ihnen sind bereits in jüdischen Familien untergebracht, da ältere arische Mädchen nicht zu bekommen sind.

Die Gerichtsurteile, die anfangs häufig sehr milde ausfielen, sind allgemein nunmehr ziemlich scharf und durchgreifend.

In Mannheim verurteilte das Gericht den jüdischen Handelsvertreter Jakob Schloss zu zwei Jahren Zuchthaus, weil er noch bis November 1935 mit einer Arierin geschlechtlich verkehrt hatte.

Wegen Betruges wurde der jüdische Bankier Weil, der rücksichtslos Erträge kleiner Bauern verspekuliert hatte, zu drei Jahren und drei Monaten Zuchthaus verurteilt.

Verhältnis zur Presse:

In der Reichspressekammer sind z.Zt. noch 13 Juden eingegliedert. Hiervon ist 2 Juden bezw. jüdischen Unternehmen das weitere Verbleiben bereits gestattet worden. Drei Anträge in dieser Hinsicht liegen noch vor. Den restlichen acht sind bereits Fristen gestellt, bis zu denen sie auszuscheiden haben.

Verhältnis zur Olympiade:

Mit gewissem Stolz wird von jüdischen Sportlern, die dem RJF nahestehen, immer wieder hervorgehoben, dass es gelungen sei, das reinrassische Frl. Bergmann in die Olympiakernmannschaft für Hochspringen zu bringen.

Verhältnis zum Ausland:

Allmählich versuchen jüdische Kreise, sich einen Rückhalt

im Ausland zu verschaffen.

Zwischen ausgewanderten Juden und zurückgebliebenen findet ein reger Briefwechsel statt, der fast durchweg in neuhebräischer Sprache geführt wird.

Zwischen den Juden diesseits und jenseits der holländischen Grenze besteht ein starker Verkehr. Ein grosser Teil der im Westen wohnenden Juden besitzt die holländische Staatsangehörigkeit; ein anderer Teil hat Grenz- und Auslandspässe.

In Österreich haben die Juden ebenfalls eine starke Stütze. Sie verlagern den Schwerpunkt ihrer Wühlarbeit dorthin und versuchen von dort aus, Deutschland unter Druck zu nehmen.

Durch Kettenbriefe suchen sie über Grenzen hinweg zum offenen Boykott deutscher Waren aufzufordern. Ein solcher Brief wurde in München aufgefunden, der seinen Ursprung in Wien genommen hatte.

Verhältnis zu den Kirchen:

Über die Teilnahme eines evangelischen Pastors an einer Gründungsversammlung des "Reichsverbandes nichtarischer Christen" wurde schon berichtet.

Besonders aus München wird immer wieder eine Zusammenarbeit von katholischen Kreisen mit Juden gemeldet. Es werden jüdischen Jugendvereinen Lokale und Plätze für ihre Betätigung zur Verfügung gestellt.

In Riesa i.Sa. hat der katholische Geistliche Rat D.theol. Rentzschka den Versuch unternommen, die vierzehnjährige Hanni Kurowski, die dem BDM angehört, als Hausmädchen an einen Juden zu vermitteln. Als das Mädchen die Annahme dieser Stelle ablehnte, schob er dem Juden eine polnische Staatsangehörige im gleichen Alter zu.

Das denkbar beste Einvernehmen besteht in Oberhausen zwischen der dortigen jüdischen Gemeinde und der katholischen Kirchengemeinde. Beide Gemeinden haben ein Abkommen geschlossen, nach welchem in Zukunft die kath. Gemeinde die jüdische Kirchensteuer erhebt. Dadurch konnten die Juden eine Beamtenstelle einsparen.

Verhältnis zu anderen Gegnern:

Über die Zusammenarbeit mit anderen staatsfeindlichen Organisationen liegen z.Zt. wenig Meldungen vor.

Nur aus Danzig wird berichtet, dass sich die deutsch-nationale Presse für jüdische Belange stark einsetzt. Vertreter jener Partei nehmen offiziell an jüdischen Heldengedenkfeiern in Synagogen teil.

+ + + + + + + + + +

50

OFFICE OF CHIEF OF COUNSEL
FOR WAR CRIMES
APO 696 - A   US ARMY

STAFF EVIDENCE ANALYSIS, MINISTRIES DIVISION

                                    By: E. Dolling
                                    Date: 14 November 1946

Document number: NG - 2612

Title and/or general nature: Ministry of the Interior
                                    legislation defining the
                                    professional status of
                                    Jewish physicians; signed
                                    by HITLER, HESS, FRICK,
                                    GUERTNER and initialled by
                                    LAMMERS.

Form of document: A) Mimeographed letter
                                    B) Mimeographed draft
                                    C) Mimeographed letter
                                    D) Mimeographed draft
                                    E) Photographic copy

Date: A) 19 May 1936
                                    B) Undated
                                    C) 9 September 1938
                                    D) Undated
                                    E) 25 July 1938

                                                            Doc. 6

Source: Reichskanzlei Akten betref-
                                    fend Juedische Angelegen-   **51**
                                    heiten im allgemeinen (595)
                                    now at: MDB, Berlin
                                    Building 30
                                    CCC PBT 3027 A,B,C,D,E

PERSONS OR ORGANIZATIONS IMPLICATED:
                                    PFUNDTNER
                                    STUCKART
                                    REINHARDT

TO BE FILED UNDER THESE REFERENCE HEADINGS:
                                    NG - Ministry of Justice
                                    NG - Political and Racial
                                         Persecution
                                    NG - Reich Chancellery
                                    NG - Ministry of Finance
                                    NG - Prussian Ministry of
                                         Interior

SUMMARY:
A)   Mimeographed cover letter dated 19 May 1936, signed by
PFUNDTNER and addressed by distribution list to top Reich
authorities, the Prussian Minister President and the Prussian
Finance Minister. Reference is made to an enclosed decree
which the Ministry of the Interior proposes to publish in
the names of all the Reich ministers, the Prussian Minister
President and the Prussian state ministers.

B)   Undated mimeographed copy of the proposed decree
providing that Germans in public offices will no longer
employ the services of Jewish physicians.

- 1 -

C)   Mimeographed cover letter signed by STUCKART and
dated 9 September 1936 re enclosed second draft of the above
decree which incorporates various changes (underlined in
enclosed copy) suggested by the Minister of Justice
(GUERTNER).

D)   Mimeographed copy of the draft with STUCKART's
typed signature provides that officials, employees and
laborers of public concerns shall not make use of the
professional services of Jewish doctors, hospitals,
mortuaries etc.

E)   Photographic copy of the fourth decree for the
implementation of the Reich Citizenship law dated 25 July 1938
initialled by LAMMERS and signed by HITLER, HESS, GUERTNER,
FRICK and REINHARDT (the last for the Minister of Finance).
Decree defines the professional status of Jewish doctors.

52

- END -

Der Reichs- und Preußische
Minister des Innern.

II SB.6403/2838.

Berlin, den .... 19.Mai 1936.
NW 40, Königsplatz 6.
Fernsprecher:
Abt. Z, I, IV, VI, VII: A 1 Jäger 0027
II, III, V (Unter den Linden 72/76): A 2 Flora 0034
Sicherheit der Dienststellen: A 2 Flora 2821 (Offizier vom Dienst)
Drahtanschrift: Innenminister.

Im Einvernehmen mit dem Herrn Reichsminister der Finanzen beabsichtige ich, den beiliegenden Runderlass zugleich im Namen sämtlicher Reichsminister, des Preußischen Ministerpräsidenten und sämtlicher Preußischen Staatsminister zu veröffentlichen, falls nicht binnen 2 Wochen Einwendungen erhoben werden.

Für die Veröffentlichung in den dortigen Amtsblättern übersende ich später einen Abdruck.

Zusatz bei:

Reichspostminister: Zu IV5820-0 vom 8.Oktober 1935.

Reichs- und Preußischen Arbeitsminister: Zu Ia 7534/35 vom 22.Januar 1936.

Reichs- und Preußischen Minister für Wissenschaft,Erziehung und Volksbildung: Zu II b 189 M, Z I vom 2.Januar 1936.

Preußischen Finanzminister: Zu I C 2500/22.10. vom 9.Dezember 1935.

Reichsfinanzminister: Zu A 5200-318/36 I B vom 2.Mai 1933.

Mit Rücksicht auf die Bedeutung der Angelegenheit für die gesamte Beamtenschaft halte ich die Veröffentlichung des Runderlasses in RMBliV. für geboten.

In Vertretung

[Unterschrift]

An

die Obersten Reichsbehörden,
den Herrn Preußischen Ministerpräsidenten,
den Herrn Preußischen Finanzminister.

53

Anlage zu II SB. 6403/2938.

NG - 2612

An die
    nachgeordneten Behörden, Gemeinden,
    Gemeindeverbände, sonst.Körperschaf-
    ten des öffentl. Rechts.

        Abdruck im RMBliV. Abschn. 1.
        Inanspruchnahme jüdischer Ärzte usw. durch Behördenangehörige
        RdErl.d.RuPrMdI. zugl.i.N. sämtl.Reichsmin., d.Pr.Min.Präs.u.
        sämtl.PrStMin. v.   1936 - II SB. 6403/2938 -.

        Mit der Pflichtauffassung eines verantwortungsbewußten
    und volksverbundenen Behördenangehörigen (Beamten, Angestell-
    ten und Arbeiters) ist es nicht vereinbar, wenn er Notstands-
    beihilfen oder Unterstützungen für Kosten beantragt, die
    durch Inanspruchnahme von jüdischen Ärzten, Zahnärzten, Apo-
    theken, Heilpersonen, Kranken- und Heilanstalten, Rechtsan-
    wälten usw. entstanden sind.

        Der Behördenangehörige kann nicht erwarten, dass solche
    Kostenbeträge bei der Bemessung der Notstandsbeihilfen oder
    Unterstützungen Berücksichtigung finden, es sei denn, dass
    ein ganz besonders gelagerter Einzelfall vorliegt, z.B. wenn
    die Zuziehung eines jüdischen Arztes bei drohender Lebensge-
    fahr unvermeidlich war.

        Zeugnisse jüdischer Ärzte können in Zukunft zum Nachweis
    der Dienstunfähigkeit nicht als ausreichend angesehen werden.

Zusatz für die Deutsche Reichsbahn-Gesellschaft und das Reichsbankdirektorium'

        Ich bitte, auch in Ihrem Geschäftsbereich entsprechend zu
    verfahren.

54

Der Reichs- und Preußische
Minister des Innern
II SB. 6403/3433

Berlin NW 40, den 9.September 1936
Königsplatz 6
3529 C

Orig. i. a. ⟨handwritten⟩ !

An

die Obersten Reichsbehörden,
(ohne Reichsjustizminister und ohne Stellvertreter des Führers)
den Herrn Preussischen Ministerpräsidenten,

den Herrn Preussischen Finanzminister.

———

Im Nachgang zu meinem Schreiben vom 19.5.1936
- II SB. 6403/2838 -

Mit seinem auch Ihnen zugesandten Schreiben
vom 28.Mai 1936 - 2150 - Ia 712/36 - hat der Herr Reichsminister der Justiz mir verschiedene Änderungen zu dem
Runderlass über Inanspruchnahme jüdischer Ärzte usw.
durch Behördenangehörige vorgeschlagen. Ich habe diese
Vorschläge in dem in Abschrift anliegenden neuen Entwurf,
soweit mir dies erforderlich schien, berücksichtigt. Die
Änderungen sind durch Unterstreichung kenntlich gemacht.
Falls nicht binnen 2 Wochen Einwendungen gegen diese
Neufassung erhoben werden, werde ich diesen Erlass ver-
öffentlichen.

In Vertretung des Staatssekretärs

⟨signature⟩

- RK 11267B

Abschrift.

Der Reichs- und Preussische

Minister des Innern

II SB. 6403/3433

An

die nachgeordneten Behörden,
Gemeinden, Gemeindeverbände,
sonst.Körperschaften des
öffentl. Rechts.

———————

56

Abdruck im RMBliV.Abschn.1

Inanspruchnahme jüdischer Ärzte usw. durch

Behördenangehörige

RdErl.d. RuPrMdI.zugl. i.N.sämtl.

Reichsmin.d.Pr.MinPräs. u. sämtl.

PrSt.Min. v.   1936 -II SB.

6403

　　　　Mit der Pflichtauffassung eines verantwortungs-
bewussten und volksverbundenen Behördenangehörigen (Beamten,
Angestellten und Arbeiters) ist es nicht vereinbar, wenn
er Notstandsbeihilfen (auch Abschlagszahlungen) oder Unterstützungen für Kosten beantragt, die durch Inanspruchnahme
von jüdischen Ärzten, Zahnärzten, Apotheken, Heilpersonen,
Kranken- und Heilanstalten, Entbindungsheimen, Beerdigungs-
instituten, Rechtsanwälten usw. entstanden sind. Wer als
Jude anzusehen ist, ergibt sich aus § 5 der Ersten Verordnung
zum Reichsbürgergesetz vom 10.11.1935 (RGBl.I S.1333).

　　　　Der Behördenangehörige kann nicht erwarten,

　　　　　　　　　　　　dass

dass solche Kostenbeträge bei der Bemessung der Notstandsbeihilfen oder Unterstützungen Berücksichtigung finden,
es sei denn, dass ein ganz besonders gelagerter Einzelfall vorliegt (z.B. wenn die Zuziehung eines jüdischen
Arztes bei drohender Lebensgefahr unvermeidlich war.).

Zeugnisse jüdischer Ärzte können in Zukunft zum
Nachweis einer dauernden oder vorübergehenden Dienstun-
fähigkeit nicht als ausreichend angesehen werden.

Der Runderlass gilt entsprechend für ehemalige Behördenangehörige und Hinterbliebene von Behördenangehörige.
Auf jüdische Beamte im Ruhestand und jüdische Hinterbliebene von Beamten ist er nicht anzuwenden.

Zusatz f.d.Deutsche Reichsbahn-Gesellschaft und
das Reichsbankdirektorium:

Ich bitte, auch in Ihrem Geschäftsbereich entsprechend zu verfahren.

In Vertretung des Staatssekretärs
gez.Dr.Stuckart.

57

Vierte Verordnung
zum Reichsbürgergesetz
vom 25. J u l i 1938.

Auf Grund des § 3 des Reichsbürgergesetzes vom 15.September 1935 (Reichsgesetzbl. I S.1146) wird folgendes verordnet:

§ 1

Bestallungen (Approbationen) jüdischer Ärzte erlöschen am 30.September 1938.

§ 2

Der Reichsminister des Innern oder die von ihm ermächtigte Stelle kann auf Vorschlag der Reichsärztekammer Ärzten, deren Bestallung auf Grund des § 1 erloschen ist, die Ausübung des Arzteberufes widerruflich gestatten. Die Genehmigung kann unter Auflagen erteilt werden.

§ 3

(1) Juden, deren Bestallung (Approbation) erloschen und denen eine Genehmigung nach § 2 nicht erteilt ist, ist es verboten, die Heilkunde auszuüben.

(2) Ein Jude, dem eine Genehmigung nach § 2 erteilt ist, darf, abgesehen von seiner Frau und seinen ehelichen Kindern, nur Juden behandeln.

(3) Wer vorsätzlich oder fahrlässig den Bestimmungen in Abs. 1 oder 2 zuwiderhandelt, wird mit Gefängnis bis zu 1 Jahr und mit Geldstrafe oder mit einer dieser Strafen bestraft.

§ 4

JFD 295

§ 4

Die Bestallung als Arzt kann einem Juden nicht erteilt werden.

§ 5

(1) Ärzten, deren Bestallung (Approbation) nach den Bestimmungen dieser Verordnung erloschen ist, kann bei Bedürftigkeit und Würdigkeit von der Reichsärztekammer ein jederzeit widerruflicher Unterhaltszuschuß gewährt werden, wenn sie Frontkämpfer gewesen sind.

(2) Das Nähere bestimmt die Reichsärztekammer im Einverständnis mit dem Reichsminister des Innern und dem Reichsminister der Finanzen.

§ 6

Dienstverträge, die ein von § 1 betroffener jüdischer Arzt als Dienstberechtigter geschlossen hat, können von beiden Teilen unter Einhaltung einer Kündigungsfrist von 6 Wochen für den 31.Dezember 1938 auch dann gekündigt werden, wenn nach den gesetzlichen oder vertraglichen Bestimmungen die Auflösung des Dienstverhältnisses erst zu einem späteren Zeitpunkt zulässig wäre. Gesetzliche oder vertragliche Bestimmungen, wonach eine Kündigung des Dienstvertrages schon zu einem früheren Zeitpunkt zulässig ist, bleiben unberührt.

§ 7

(1) Auf die Kündigung von Mietverhältnissen über Räume, die ein durch § 1 betroffener jüdischer Arzt für sich, seine Familie oder für seine Berufsausübung gemietet

hat,

hat, finden die Vorschriften des Gesetzes über das Kündigungsrecht der durch das Gesetz zur Wiederherstellung des Berufsbeamtentums betroffenen Personen vom 7.April 1933 (Reichsgesetzbl. I S.187), im Lande Österreich die Vorschriften des § 13 der Verordnung zur Neuordnung des österreichischen Berufsbeamtentums vom 31.Mai 1938 (RGBl. I S.607) entsprechende Anwendung. Die Kündigung muß für den 30.September 1938 erfolgen und dem Vermieter spätestens am ~~31.Juli~~ 1938 zugehen. Ein Widerspruch des Vermieters gegen die Kündigung ist unzulässig, wenn dem Vermieter durch die Reichsärztekammer oder die von ihr bestimmte Stelle ein anderer ärztlicher Mieter nachgewiesen wird.

(2) Der Vermieter kann das Mietverhältnis unter den gleichen Voraussetzungen innerhalb der gleichen Frist kündigen. Dem Mieter steht ein Widerspruchsrecht nicht zu.

(3) Die Vorschriften des Abs. 1 Satz 1 gelten entsprechend für Dienstverpflichtete von jüdischen Ärzten, wenn sie infolge des Erlöschens der Bestallung (Approbation) des Dienstberechtigten stellungslos geworden sind.

(4) Der Reichsminister des Innern wird ermächtigt, im Einvernehmen mit dem Reichsminister der Justiz durch Verordnung Bestimmungen über die Auflösung von Mietverhältnissen über die in Abs. 1 genannten Räumlichkeiten zu treffen.

§ 8

Der Reichsminister des Innern wird ermächtigt, die Reichs-Ärzteordnung vom 13.Dezember 1935 (Reichsgesetzbl. I S. 1433)

durch

durch Bekanntmachung entsprechend abzuändern.

Bayreuth, den 25. Juli 1938.

Der Führer und Reichskanzler

[signature]

Der Reichsminister des Innern

[signature: Frick]

Der Stellvertreter des Führers

[signature: R. Heß]

Der Reichsminister der Justiz

[signature: Dr. Gürtner]

Der Reichsminister der Finanzen

In Vertretung

[signature]

JPD 208

NOTE

A Copy of <u>Reichgesetzblatt</u>, Part 1, No. 122
with the Fourth Regulation to the Reich Citizenship Law was left with the report, summary
and translation in order to preserve the
continuity of the document.

The Editor

Doc. 7

DOCUMENT FILE

NOTE

SEE ___862.1281/89_____ FOR ___Despatch #288_____

FROM _____Germany_____(Wilson)_____) DATED ___August 13, 1938___

TO   **NAME**   1—1127   •••

REGARDING: race problems- Germany. Translation of law terminating as of September 30,1938, validity of licenses to practice held by Jewish physicians. Survey of number of doctors to be effected by the law as given in the VOLKISCHER BEOBACHTER of August 4.

63

fp

Berlin, August 13, 1938.

No. 238

SUBJECT: The Jewish Situation, with Particular
Reference to the Exclusion of Jewish
Doctors from Practice.

The Honorable

The Secretary of State,

Washington.

Sir:

Referring to the Embassy's telegrams No. 372
of August 3, 5 p.m., and No. 374 of August 4, 4 p.m., I
have the honor to enclose copies of REICHSGESETZBLATT,
Part I, No. 122 of August 2, 1938, containing a law which
terminates as of September 30, 1938, the validity of
licenses to practice held by Jewish physicians. An English
translation of this law is also enclosed.

The VOELKISCHER BEOBACHTER of August 4 presented
a survey of the number of doctors who will be affected by

the

the law. It explained that at the beginning of 1933 there
were 6,480 Jewish doctors in Germany, including the "non-
Aryan" crossbreeds and those with Jewish wives (the latter
two categories, however, being numerically unimportant inasmuch as most of the Jewish doctors were full-blooded Jews).
In the old Reich territory there are at present 4,220 Jewish
doctors, 3,748 of whom actively engage in practice. The
total number of doctors in the old Reich territory is given
as 37,525, the Jews therefore representing roughly 10 percent
of this figure. As of July of this year there were 6,949
doctors in Berlin, 1,561, or 22.4 percent of whom were Jews.
Despite the steps hitherto taken to eject Jewish doctors
from the more profitable of the various State sickness insurance institutions (see despatch No. 3832 of January 17,
1938), it would appear from the VOELKISCHER BEOBACHTER'S
survey that 816 Jewish doctors still work for these organizations in Berlin. The VOELKISCHER BEOBACHTER makes no
attempt to describe the situation in Austria beyond mentioning that the proportion of Jewish physicians in Vienna is
probably still greater.

It has been an open secret for a long time that
the National Socialist authorities have been determined to
exclude Jewish doctors, but have until now refrained from
doing so for fear of creating a shortage of physicians when
they were particularly needed to meet the requirements of a
greatly expanded army. Even with the entry into practice of

the

65

the new corps of young doctors who have been pressed into
service with abbreviated periods of training, it would seem
doubtful whether the sweeping removal of 22.4 percent of the
doctors in Berlin, for instance, will not create a serious
shortage.

Official commentaries explain that the licenses
which henceforth will be granted certain Jewish doctors by way
of exception will be issued only to a limited number of physicians to enable them to care for Jewish patients in cities
where numerous and compact concentrations of Jews are to be
found, as in Berlin and Vienna. The provisions in the law
with respect to the summary denunciation of rent contracts is
interesting. On the one hand it seems designed to assist
Jewish doctors to free themselves from leases likely to prove
onerous in view of the curtailment of their incomes. On the
other hand it also enables landlords to rid themselves of
Jewish tenants. This they are invited to do by the Berlin
association of house-owners which explains that a shortage
of premises has been a detriment in the past to "Aryan" doctors.
The association requests landlords to inform it of possible
vacancies which it in turn will endeavor to fill with "Aryan"
doctors.

The preamble to the DEUTSCHES NACHRICHTEN BÜRO
announcement of the enactment of the doctors law is worthy of
note. It states: "The Jewish question in Germany will be
solved step by step, but resolutely, by legal ways." The
proof of this assertion may be found in the recent and
progressive exclusion of Jews from a number of professions such
as watchman's services, private detective work, trading in

real

real estate, etc., (see Embassy's despatch No. 246, of
July 16, 1938). Incidentally the law canceling the licenses
of Jews to engage in itinerant trades is being employed to
deny them activity as travelling salesmen and commercial
agents. The approximate coincidence of all these measures
with the meeting and conclusion of the Evian Refugee Conference
is perhaps too striking to necessitate further comment.

At present wide circulation is being given to
extraordinary stories with respect to conditions in the new
concentration camp at Buchenwald near Weimar where it is
estimated that some 1,500 Jews are being detained (see Embassy's despatch No. 196 of June 22, 1938). While some of
these stories appear somewhat extreme, such as the report
that Jewish victims are being utilized to test the efficacy
of new poison gases, the accounts of relatives of inmates
and released prisoners seem to indicate that brutality and
sadism are being practiced by the guards on a scale that
has not been equalled since the early days of the regime in
1933. That the primary purpose of the camp is to encourage
emigration rather than to punish specific delicts, is evi-
dent from statements received at the Consulate General from
persons who have been released with the warning that if
they did not leave the country by a certain date they would
be reincarcerated. It is not too much to say that the apparently indiscriminate arrests without specific cause has
created a state of near terror in many Jewish circles.

In accordance with the Department's circular
instruction of July 21, 1938, two copies of this despatch

are

67

- 5 -

are being sent to the American Embassy, London, for the attention of the American Representative on the Intergovernmental Committee for Political Refugees.

Respectfully yours,

Hugh R. Wilson.

68

Enclosures:
1. REICHSGESETZBLATT I, 122
2. Translation of law.

File 800
JDB-MJP

Enclosure

Translation
REICHSGESETZBLATT, Part I, No. 122,
of August 2, 1938.

Fourth Decree of July 25, 1938, Relating to the Reich Citizenship Law.

On the basis of Section 3 of the Reich Citizenship
Law of September 15, 1935 (REICHSGESETZBLATT, Part I,
p.1146) the following is decreed:

Section 1.

Licenses (Bestallungen) of Jewish physicians terminate
as of September 30, 1938.

Section 2.

The Reich Minister of the Interior or the office
empowered by him may on the proposal of the Reich
Chamber of Physicians permit physicians, whose licenses
have terminated on the basis of Section 1, to practice
the profession of medicine until further notice. The approval may be made subject to conditions.

Section 3.

(1) Jews whose licenses have terminated and to
whom a permit in accordance with Section 2 has not been
granted are forbidden to practice the art of healing
(Heilkunde).

(2) A Jew who has been granted a permit in accordance with Section 2 may, aside from his wife and his
children born in wedlock, treat only Jews.

(3) Whoever deliberately or unwittingly contravenes the regulations in Par. (1) or (2) will be punished
with imprisonment up to one year and a fine, or by one
of these penalties.

Section

69

Section 4.

A license as physician cannot be issued to a Jew.

Section 5.

(1) Physicians whose licenses are terminated in accordance with the regulations of this decree may be granted in case of need and worthiness, and if they have been front-line fighters, a contribution toward their support, revocable at any time, by the Reich Chamber of Physicians.

(2) Details are to be determined by the Reich Chamber of Physicians in agreement with the Reich Minister of the Interior and the Reich Minister of Finance.

Section 6.

Contracts for services which a Jewish physician affected by Section 1 has concluded as the party entitled to the service may be terminated by both parties as of December 31, 1938, six weeks' notice having been given, even if according to the legal or contractual regulations the termination of the contract would be permissible only at a later date. Legal or contractual regulations according to which the termination of such a contract is permissible at an earlier date remain unaffected.

Section 7.

(1) To the termination of rent contracts for premises which a Jewish physician affected by Section 1 has rented for himself, his family or for the practice of his profession, the regulations of the law concerning the right to give notice of those persons affected

by

by the Law for the Reestablishment of the Civil
Service of April 7, 1933 (REICHSGESETZBLATT Part I,
p.187), in Austria the regulations of Section 13
of the Decree for the Reorganization of the Austrian
Civil Service of May 31, 1938 (REICHSGESETZBLATT, Part I,
p.607), apply accordingly. Notice of termination must
be given as of September 30, and must reach the landlord
by August 15, 1938, at the latest. Objection on the
part of the landlord to such notice is not permissible
if the landlord is offered another physician as tenant
by the Reich Chamber of Physicians or the office
determined by it.

(2) The landlord can give notice of termination
on the same conditions and with the same dates. The
tenant has no right to object.

(3) The regulations of paragraph (1), sentence
1, apply correspondingly to those under contract to
render services to Jewish physicians if they have lost
their positions as a result of the termination of the
license of the person entitled to such service.

(4) The Reich Minister of the Interior is authorized to issue regulations in agreement with the Reich
Minister of Justice in the form of decree concerning
the termination of rental contracts for the premises
mentioned in paragraph (1).

Section 8.

The Reich Minister of the Interior is authorized
to alter accordingly by public notice the Reich Physicians Statute of December 13, 1935 (REICHSGESETZBLATT,
Part I, p.1433).

Bayreuth, July 25, 1938.

71

Reichsgesetzblatt

Teil I

| 1938 | Ausgegeben zu Berlin, den 2. August 1938 | Nr. 122 |

72

Gesetz zur Ordnung des Marktes für Getreide, Hülsenfrüchte und Futtermittel.
Vom 31. Juli 1938.

Die Reichsregierung hat das folgende Gesetz beschlossen, das hiermit verkündet wird:

Der Reichsminister der Finanzen wird ermächtigt, zur Ordnung des Marktes für Getreide, Hülsenfrüchte und Futtermittel weitere Garantien bis zum Höchstbetrage von 250 Millionen Reichsmark zu übernehmen.

Breslau, den 31. Juli 1938.

Der Führer und Reichskanzler
Adolf Hitler

Der Reichsminister der Finanzen
Graf Schwerin von Krosigk

Der Reichsminister für Ernährung und Landwirtschaft
In Vertretung
H. Backe

Vierte Verordnung zum Reichsbürgergesetz.
Vom 25. Juli 1938.

Auf Grund des § 3 des Reichsbürgergesetzes vom 15. September 1935 (Reichsgesetzbl. I S. 1146) wird folgendes verordnet:

§ 1

Bestallungen (Approbationen) jüdischer Ärzte erlöschen am 30. September 1938.

§ 2

Der Reichsminister des Innern oder die von ihm ermächtigte Stelle kann auf Vorschlag der Reichsärztekammer Ärzten, deren Bestallung auf Grund des § 1 erloschen ist, die Ausübung des Ärzteberufes widerruflich gestatten. Die Genehmigung kann unter Auflagen erteilt werden.

§ 3

(1) Juden, deren Bestallung (Approbation) erloschen und denen eine Genehmigung nach § 2 nicht erteilt ist, ist es verboten, die Heilkunde auszuüben.

(2) Ein Jude, dem eine Genehmigung nach § 2 erteilt ist, darf, abgesehen von seiner Frau und seinen ehelichen Kindern, nur Juden behandeln.

(3) Wer vorsätzlich oder fahrlässig den Bestimmungen im Abs. 1 oder 2 zuwiderhandelt, wird mit Gefängnis bis zu einem Jahr und mit Geldstrafe oder mit einer dieser Strafen bestraft.

§ 4

Die Bestallung als Arzt kann einem Juden nicht erteilt werden.

§ 5

(1) Ärzten, deren Bestallung (Approbation) nach den Bestimmungen dieser Verordnung erloschen ist, kann bei Bedürftigkeit und Würdigkeit von der Reichsärztekammer ein jederzeit widerruflicher Unterhaltszuschuß gewährt werden, wenn sie Frontkämpfer gewesen sind.

(2) Das Nähere bestimmt die Reichsärztekammer im Einverständnis mit dem Reichsminister des Innern und dem Reichsminister der Finanzen.

§ 6

Dienstverträge, die ein von § 1 betroffener jüdischer Arzt als Dienstberechtigter geschlossen hat, können von beiden Teilen unter Einhaltung einer Kündigungsfrist von sechs Wochen für den 31. Dezember 1938 auch dann gekündigt werden, wenn nach den gesetzlichen oder vertraglichen Bestimmungen die Auflösung des Dienstverhältnisses erst zu einem späteren Zeitpunkt zulässig wäre. Gesetzliche oder vertragliche Bestimmungen, wonach eine Kündigung des Dienstvertrags schon zu einem früheren Zeitpunkt zulässig ist, bleiben unberührt.

§ 7

(1) Auf die Kündigung von Mietverhältnissen über Räume, die ein durch § 1 betroffener jüdischer Arzt für sich, seine Familie oder für seine Berufsausübung gemietet hat, finden die Vorschriften des Gesetzes über das Kündigungsrecht der durch das Gesetz zur Wiederherstellung des Berufsbeamtentums betroffenen Personen vom 7. April 1933 (Reichsgesetzbl. I S. 187), im Lande Österreich die Vorschriften des § 13 der Verordnung zur Neuordnung des österreichischen Berufsbeamtentums vom 31. Mai 1938 (Reichsgesetzbl. I S. 607) entsprechende Anwendung. Die Kündigung muß für den 30. September 1938 erfolgen und dem Vermieter spätestens am 15. August 1938 zugehen. Ein Widerspruch des Vermieters gegen die Kündigung ist unzulässig, wenn dem Vermieter durch die Reichsärztekammer oder die von ihr bestimmte Stelle ein anderer ärztlicher Mieter nachgewiesen wird.

(2) Der Vermieter kann das Mietverhältnis unter den gleichen Voraussetzungen innerhalb der gleichen Frist kündigen. Dem Mieter steht ein Widerspruchsrecht nicht zu.

(3) Die Vorschriften des Abs. 1 Satz 1 gelten entsprechend für Dienstverpflichtete von jüdischen Ärzten, wenn sie infolge des Erlöschens der Bestallung (Approbation) des Dienstberechtigten stellungslos geworden sind.

(4) Der Reichsminister des Innern wird ermächtigt, im Einvernehmen mit dem Reichsminister der Justiz durch Verordnung Bestimmungen über die Auflösung von Mietverhältnissen über die im Abs. 1 genannten Räumlichkeiten zu treffen.

73

§ 8

Der Reichsminister des Innern wird ermächtigt, die Reichsärzteordnung vom 13. Dezember 1935 (Reichsgesetzbl. I S. 1433) durch Bekanntmachung entsprechend abzuändern.

Bayreuth, den 25. Juli 1938.

Der Führer und Reichskanzler
Adolf Hitler

Der Reichsminister des Innern
Frick

Der Stellvertreter des Führers
R. Heß

Der Reichsminister der Justiz
Dr. Gürtner

Der Reichsminister der Finanzen
In Vertretung
Reinhardt

74

Fünfte Verordnung
zur Ergänzung der Verordnung über Abrechnungsstellen im Wechsel= und Scheckverkehr.
Vom 30. Juli 1938.

Auf Grund des Artikels 38 Abs. 3 des Wechselgesetzes vom 21. Juni 1933 (Reichsgesetzbl. I S. 399) und des Artikels 31 Abs. 2 des Scheckgesetzes vom 14. August 1933 (Reichsgesetzbl. I S. 597) wird zur Ergänzung der Verordnung über Abrechnungsstellen im Wechsel- und Scheckverkehr vom 14. Juni 1935 (Reichsgesetzbl. I S. 747) verordnet:

Als Abrechnungsstelle im Sinne des Artikels 38 Abs. 2 des Wechselgesetzes und des Artikels 31 Abs. 1 des Scheckgesetzes ist ferner die Abrechnungsstelle bei der Reichsbanknebenstelle Hirschberg (Schles.) anzusehen.

Die Einlieferung von Wechseln und Schecks in diese Abrechnungsstelle kann nur erfolgen, wenn der Bezogene oder die Zahlstelle Mitglied der Abrechnungsstelle ist oder bei ihr durch ein Mitglied vertreten ist.

Die Einlieferungen müssen den für den Geschäftsverkehr der Abrechnungsstelle maßgebenden Bestimmungen entsprechen.

Berlin, den 30. Juli 1938.

Der Reichsminister der Justiz
In Vertretung
Dr. Schlegelberger

Verordnung über die
Aufhebung von Durchführungsbestimmungen zur Wohlfahrtshilfeverordnung*)
Vom 1. August 1938

Auf Grund der Wohlfahrtshilfeverordnung vom 14. Juni 1932 Artikel 2 §§ 5 und 13 (Reichsgesetzbl. I S. 278) in der Fassung des Artikels 5 des Gesetzes zur Änderung und Ergänzung von Vorschriften auf dem Gebiete des Finanzwesens vom 23. März 1934 (Reichsgesetzbl. I S. 232) wird hierdurch verordnet:

Mit sofortiger Wirkung werden aufgehoben:

1. die Durchführungsbestimmungen zur Wohlfahrtshilfeverordnung vom 15. Juni 1932 (Reichsgesetzbl. I S. 303),

2. die Weiteren Durchführungsbestimmungen zur Wohlfahrtshilfeverordnung vom 2. August 1932 (Reichsgesetzbl. I S. 395),

3. die Dritten Durchführungsbestimmungen zur Wohlfahrtshilfeverordnung vom 3. November 1932 (Reichsgesetzbl. I S. 524),

4. die Vierte Durchführungsbestimmung zur Wohlfahrtshilfeverordnung vom 30. November 1932 (Reichsgesetzbl. I S. 540),

5. die Fünfte Durchführungsbestimmung zur Wohlfahrtshilfeverordnung vom 12. September 1933 (Reichsgesetzbl. I S. 623).

Berlin, 1. August 1938

Der Reichsminister der Finanzen
In Vertretung
Reinhardt

Der Reichsarbeitsminister
In Vertretung des Staatssekretärs
Rettig

---

*) Betrifft nicht das Land Österreich.

(1

OFFICE OF CHIEF OF COUNSEL
FOR WAR CRIMES
APO 696-A   U.S.ARMY

STAFF EVIDENCE ANALYSIS, Ministries Division.

By Dr. Mosse
Date: 31 March 1947

Document Number: NG - 1261

Title and/or general nature:Elimination of Jewish Members
                            from the "Association for Art
                            History".

Form of Document: Typewritten carbon copy of a
                           report

Stamps and other endorsments:Signature of ZSCHINTZSCH

Date: 17 March 1938

Source: Reich Ministry of Education
                           folder "Staatssecretar ZSCHINT
                           TZSCH   M.I.
                           now at: MDB, Berlin,
                           Building II
                           (OCC BET 1414)

PERSONS OR ORGANIZATIONS IMPLICATED:
                           ZSCHINTZSCH

TO BE FILMED UNDER THESE REFERENCE HEADINGS:
                           NG - Ministry of Education

Doc. 8

75

SUMMARY:

     This report to RUST concerns a disagreement between
ZSCHINTZSCH and the chief of division V of his Ministry.
(Analyst's note: The report of the chief of division V is
not available).
     In 1934, the Ministry ordered the "Association for Art
History" to drop its Jewish members. The Association did
not comply with that order and reported only on the coordi-
nation (Gleichschaltung) of its board of directors. The
Ministry intended to go back to this matter in due time.
ZSCHINTZSCH holds that now the Association has to get a
clear answer to its letter of 22.1.1938. It has to be
informed that an association could not have the title of
"German Association for Art History" while, at the same time,
tolerating Jews among its members. Under no circumstances
an association with Jewish members may expect any assistance
from the state. Contrary to the opinion of the chief of
division V, ZSCHINTZSCH deems the Minister to be entitled to
issue such information without regard to the legal situation
viz. since
a) in the years of 1934 and 1935, the Minister had a corres-
    pondence concerning this matter with the Association,
b) the Association asks for subsidy from the state,
c) the Minister has to see to it that the Association will
    finally comply with the principles of the National So-
    cialist creed.

Dem

Herrn M i n i s t e r

mit anliegendem Vermerk des Herrn Amtschefs V, in dem er einer
von mir vertretenen Auffassung nicht folgt, weitergeleitet.

Ich habe dazu zu bemerken:

1) Ich bin allerdings der Auffassung, daß ein Amtschef oder
ein Referent des Hauses, der im Verlauf seiner Tätigkeit sich
mit irgendeiner Angelegenheit zu beschäftigen hat, wie im vorliegenden Falle mit dem Verein für Kunstwissenschaft, die
Pflicht hat, sich aus den Akten des Ministeriums ein vollstän-
diges Bild über die Angelegenheit zu machen, ehe er mit außen-
stehenden Personen in Besprechungen tritt. Das ist im vorliegenden Falle nicht geschehen. Aus den Akten ging klar hervor,
daß im August 1934 von dem Verein die Einführung eines Arierpara-
graphen verlangt war. Diesem Verlangen hat der Verein nicht
entsprochen, sondern lediglich angezeigt, daß er „eine Gleichschaltung im Vorstande" vorgenommen habe. Dieses Verfahren
ist vom Ministerium dadurch gebilligt worden, daß davon Kenntnis
genommen worden ist und man sich vorbehalten hat, zu gegebener
Zeit auf die Angelegenheit zurückzukommen.

Aus den Akten geht weiter klar hervor, daß die weitere
Herausgabe des Werkes von Frankl und Julius Baum (beide Juden)
durch den Verein für Kunstwissenschaft vom Ministerium ausdrücklich gebilligt worden ist.

Hätte der Amtschef V, sich hinreichend durch seinen Referenten
über diesen, wie ich zugebe bedauerlichen, aber nun einmal
bestehenden Sachverhalt informiert, hätte er keine Überraschun-
gen erlebt.

./.

2) Der Amtsohef V hat mich in zwei Punkten mißverstanden:
Ich will den Verein wegen seines Verhaltens keineswegs in Schutz
nehmen. Ich will auch nicht in Schutz nehmen den Schriftführer
Meyer, der Graf Baudissin bei einer Besprechung nicht vollstän-
dig unterrichtet hat. Ich glaube aber, daß das Verhalten des
Herrn Meyer, der nach meiner Auffassung (vgl. Ziff.1) voraus-
setzen konnte, daß der Amtsohef V unterrichtet war, nicht so
schwerwiegend zu verurteilen ist, als daß er aus seinem staatlichen Angestelltenverhältnis entlassen werden müßte.

3) Ich halte es für falsch, dem Verein eine Warnung dadurch
erteilen zu wollen, daß sein Schriftführer aus seinem staatlichen
Anstellungsverhältnis entlassen wird. Ich bin vielmehr der
Auffassung, daß dem Verein auf sein letztes Schreiben vom
22. Januar 1938 hin eine unmißverständliche Äußerung zugehen
muß, etwa des Inhalts, daß ein Verein den Namen „Deutscher
Verein für Kunstwissenschaft" nicht führen kann, wenn er Juden
in seinen Reihen hat, daß ein Verein mit jüdischen Mitgliedern
unter keinen Umständen auf staatliche Förderung rechnen kann
und daß schließlich es nicht gebilligt werden kann, wenn Staats-
beamte diesem Verein als Vorstandsmitglieder oder auch als einfache Mitglieder weiterhin angehören.

Im Gegensatz zum Amtsohef halte ich den Minister zu einer
solchen Mitteilung durchaus für befugt, ganz gleichgültig wie
die Rechtslage ist, weil
a) der Minister im Jahre 1934 und 1935 mit dem Verein über die
   gleiche Angelegenheit einen Schriftwechsel geführt hat,
b) der Verein eine staatliche Unterstützung erstrebt,

c)

77

c) der Minister ein Interesse daran haben muß, daß der
   Verein endlich den Grundsätzen nationalsozialistischer
   Auffassung entspricht.

Ein Heft, aus dem sich der Akteninhalt über den Verein
ergibt, ist beigefügt.

            Berlin, den 17. März 1938.

78

DEPARTMENT OF STATE

DIVISION OF EUROPEAN AFFAIRS

The law is deplored as discriminatory, if taken in relation to the position of other religious communities and may hamper the social and welfare work of the Jewish communities in Germany.

EU: Flack.

DEPARTMENT OF STATE

DIVISION OF EUROPEAN AFFAIRS

April 15, 1938.

Summary of despatch No. 74 from the Embassy at Berlin, dated April 5/38.

Subject: New Legal Status of Jewish Communities.

According to a new law of March 30, 1938, Jewish religious communities have been deprived of the semi-public status they have enjoyed as "Corporations Under Public Law". This new law in theory reduces the Jewish communities in Germany to the private status they occupy in other countries.

According to authoritative Jewish sources the Jewish communities in Germany have until now possessed in each city privileges in some respects similar to the established Churches in Germany, receiving protection from the state and being able to depend upon the state to collect taxes for the support of their religious welfare and activities.

As a result of the new law the Jewish communities now become merely private bodies with a status similar to that of other duly registered associations.

862.4016/1709

EMBASSY OF THE
UNITED STATES OF AMERICA

Berlin, April 5, 1938

No. 74

Subject: New Legal Status of the Jewish
Communities.

The Honorable

The Secretary of State,

Washington.

Sir:

      I have the honor to enclose a copy of REICHS-
GESETZBLATT Part I, No. 45, of March 30, 1938, containing a law depriving the Jewish religious communities of the semi-public status they have enjoyed
as "corporations under public law" (Körperschaften des
öffentlichen Rechts) and reducing them to the position

of

of private societies. An English translation of this
law is likewise enclosed.

According to information received from authoritative Jewish sources, the Jewish religious communities,
or Gemeinde, have until now possessed in each city
privileges in some respects similar to the established
churches, receiving protection from the State and being
able to depend upon the State to collect taxes for the
support of their religious and welfare activities. In
the same sense that the Catholic and Protestant clergy
are regarded as State officials, the Jewish Rabbis also
enjoyed that privilege. As a result of the law referred
to above, the Jewish communities now become merely private bodies with a status similar to that of other
duly registered associations (eingetragene Vereine) or
clubs.

It is provided that this change shall take place
as of March 31. It may be noted that the law is considered to have become law last January 1, but by virtue
of the fact that it was only promulgated March 30, the
Jewish communities have thus been deprived of a three
months' period of notice which might have made it easier
for them to adjust themselves to the new arrangement.
Application of the law to Austria remains for the time
being in abeyance.

As judged by local Jewish authorities, the law
may have the following effects. The Jewish Gemeinde

may

82

may no longer receive, as of official right, the
taxes levied upon their members by the State for the
meeting of community expenses, such as the Rabbis'
salaries, the upkeep of synagogues, Jewish schools and
hospitals, relief work, old age pensions of contribut-
ing members and the payment of the salaries and pensions
of officials of the community. It is understood, however, that it has been intimated to the officials of
the Jewish communities that they may bring civil suit
against non-paying members, just as certain other
private associations and clubs are entitled to bring
suit for the non-payment of dues. With the former
legal basis removed whereby contributions were collected
as State taxes, it is feared in some quarters that many
members of the Jewish communities, particularly in the
degree that they may suffer from the pressure of official
and Party economic discrimination, may refuse to pay
their contributions voluntarily, and it is perceived that
the collection of these contributions by court process
would be a costly procedure. On the other hand, certain
other Jewish authorities rely upon the esprit de corps
of the Jewish community members to induce them to continue to pay as contributions the sums they formerly
paid as assessed taxes. It may be regarded as of some
significance, however, that the competent Government
officials have stated that they will refuse to divulge
the sums formerly paid to the communities by individual
members as taxes which in turn were based upon a pro-

portion

- 4 -

portion of the total income tax paid to the State.

Officials of the local Jewish community perceive that the law may work another hardship in that, following the termination of their public status, the communities may be called upon to pay taxes upon their property such as synagogues, cemeteries, administrative buildings, and so forth. Certain of the communities are understood, moreover, to possess archives and art collections of historic and intrinsic value, but they may not sell these (in order, possibly, to meet rising current expenses) without the permission of the Government.

While the new law in theory reduces the Jewish communities in Germany to the private status they occupy in other countries, it is nevertheless deplored as discriminatory, if taken in relation to the position that the other religious communities enjoy as established churches, and it is counted upon to hamper, to a degree that may possibly be very great, the social and welfare work of the already seriously harassed Jewish Gemeinde.

Respectfully yours,

Hugh R. Wilson.

Enclosures:

1. Copy of REICHSGESETZBLATT *in dupl.*
   Part I, No.45, of March 30,
   1938;
2. Translation of Law.

800
JDB-gw

83

Translation
from
REICHSGESETZBLATT, Part I, No.45
March 30, 1938.

Law Governing the Legal Status of
Jewish Religious Associations.

Of March 28, 1938.

The Reich Government has passed the following law,
which is promulgated herewith:

Section 1.

(1) Jewish religious associations (Kultusvereinigungen)
and their societies obtain legal competence by entry in
the register of societies.

(2) Upon the expiration of March 31, 1938, the Jewish religious associations and their societies lose the
position of corporations (Körperschaften des öffentlichen
Rechts), if they have possessed it hitherto. From that
date on they are societies endowed with legal personality
under civil law. Entry in the register of societies must
be effected subsequently.

Section 2.

The officers of the associations and societies mentioned in Section 1, par.2, lose their capacity as officers upon the expiration of March 31, 1938. On the
same date they enter into an official relationship to
the associations and societies based on civil law, to
which the former adjustment of their rights and duties
applies mutatis mutandis.

Section 3.

(1) Approval of the high administrative authority
is required by:

Decisions

Decisions of the organs of the Jewish religious
associations and their societies

   a) when forming, changing and dissolving the
      associations and societies;

   b) when selling or substantially changing articles
      which have a historical, scientific or artistic
      value, especially archives or parts thereof.

(2) The high administrative authority can protest
against the appointment of members of the organs of the
Jewish religious associations and their societies.

Section 4.

The Reich Minister for Church Affairs, in concurrence
with the Reich Minister of the Interior, may issue legal
and administrative regulations for the execution and supplementation of this law.

Section 5.

(1)This law goes into effect as of January 1, 1938.

(2)On this date contradictory regulations become null
and void.

(3)The right to apply this law to the Province of
Austria is reserved.

Berlin, March 28, 1938.

               The Führer and Reich Chancelor
                    Adolf Hitler

               The Reich Minister for Church Affairs
                    Kerrl

               The Reich Minister of the Interior
                    Frick

AC-GW

85

Reichsgesetzblatt

Teil I

1938	Ausgegeben zu Berlin, den 30. März 1938	Nr. 45

86

Zweites Gesetz zur Änderung der Vorschriften über die Gebäudeentschuldungsteuer
Vom 28. März 1938

Die Reichsregierung hat das folgende Gesetz beschlossen, das hierdurch verkündet wird:

§ 1

Grundbesitz, der der Nationalsozialistischen Deutschen Arbeiterpartei oder den im § 4 Ziffer 2 des Grundsteuergesetzes vom 1. Dezember 1936 (Reichsgesetzbl. I S. 986) genannten Verbänden gehört oder von ihnen benutzt wird, ist ab 1. April 1938 von der Gebäudeentschuldungsteuer in dem Umfang befreit, in dem er von der Grundsteuer befreit ist.

§ 2

Das Gesetz über die Befreiung des Grundbesitzes der Nationalsozialistischen Deutschen Arbeiterpartei von der Grundsteuer und der Gebäudeentschuldungsteuer vom 15. April 1935 (Reichsgesetzbl. I S. 508) tritt am 1. April 1938 außer Kraft.

§ 3

Die obersten Landesbehörden werden ermächtigt, mit Zustimmung des Reichsministers der Finanzen die landesrechtlichen Vorschriften über die Gebäudeentschuldungsteuer an die Vorschriften des Grundsteuergesetzes anzugleichen.

Berlin, 28. März 1938

Der Führer und Reichskanzler
Adolf Hitler

Der Reichsminister der Finanzen
Graf Schwerin von Krosigk

Geſetz über die Rechtsverhältniſſe der jüdiſchen Kultusvereinigungen.
Vom 28. März 1938.

Die Reichsregierung hat das folgende Geſetz beſchloſſen, das hiermit verkündet wird:

§ 1

(1) Die jüdiſchen Kultusvereinigungen und ihre Verbände erlangen die Rechtsfähigkeit durch Eintragung in das Vereinsregiſter.

(2) Mit Ablauf des 31. März 1938 verlieren die jüdiſchen Kultusvereinigungen und ihre Verbände die Stellung von Körperſchaften des öffentlichen Rechts, ſoweit ſie dieſe bisher beſaßen. Sie ſind von dieſem Zeitpunkt an rechtsfähige Vereine des bürgerlichen Rechts. Die Eintragung in das Vereinsregiſter iſt nachzuholen.

§ 2

Die Beamten der im § 1 Abſ. 2 genannten Vereinigungen und Verbände verlieren mit Ablauf des 31. März 1938 ihre Beamteneigenſchaft. Sie treten mit demſelben Zeitpunkt zu den Vereinigungen und Verbänden in ein bürgerlich-rechtliches Dienſtverhältnis, auf das die bisherige Regelung ihrer Rechte und Pflichten entſprechende Anwendung findet.

§ 3

(1) Der Genehmigung durch die höhere Verwaltungsbehörde bedürfen:

Beſchlüſſe der Organe der jüdiſchen Kultusvereinigungen und ihrer Verbände

a) bei Bildung, Veränderung und Auflöſung der Vereinigungen und Verbände,

b) bei Veräußerungen oder weſentlichen Veränderungen von Gegenſtänden, die einen geſchichtlichen, wiſſenſchaftlichen oder Kunſtwert haben, insbeſondere von Archiven oder Teilen von ſolchen.

(2) Die höhere Verwaltungsbehörde kann gegen die Berufung der Mitglieder der Organe der jüdiſchen Kultusvereinigungen und ihrer Verbände Einſpruch erheben.

§ 4

Der Reichsminiſter für die kirchlichen Angelegenheiten kann zur Durchführung und Ergänzung dieſes Geſetzes im Einvernehmen mit dem Reichsminiſter des Innern Rechts- und Verwaltungsvorſchriften erlaſſen.

§ 5

(1) Das Geſetz tritt mit Wirkung vom 1. Januar 1938 in Kraft.

(2) Mit dieſem Zeitpunkt treten entgegenſtehende Beſtimmungen außer Kraft.

(3) Die Inkraftſetzung dieſes Geſetzes für das Land Öſterreich bleibt vorbehalten.

Berlin, den 28. März 1938.

Der Führer und Reichskanzler
Adolf Hitler

Der Reichsminiſter für die kirchlichen Angelegenheiten
Kerrl

Der Reichsminiſter des Innern
Frick

87

STAFF EVIDENCE ANALYSIS, Ministries Division.

By: Mark Schafer
Date: 10 April 1947

Document Number: NG-1413

Title   and/or general nature: Dossier on the treatment of
                                     American Jews in Germany,
                                     containing original drafts of
                                     negative replies by WEIZSAECKER
                                     to protest notes by the American
                                     charge d'affaires over
                                     discrimination against American
                                     citizens, resident in Germany,
                                     for reasons of race and creed.

Form of Document: Dossier

Stamps and other endorsements: Initials and corrections by
                                     WEIZSAECKER.

Date: 9 May 1938 to 27 December 1938

Source: "Auswaertiges Amt, Buero des
                                     Staatssekretaers betreffend USA.
                                     Frame Nos. Bоо4928-Воо5873/3";
                                     now at: FO-SD, Building 32, MDB,
                                     Berlin.
                                     (OCC BBT,1066)

Doc. 10

88

PERSONS OR ORGANIZATIONS IMPLICATED:
                                     WEIZSAECKER
                                     WOERMANN
                                     THOMSEN

TO BE FILED UNDER THESE REFERENCE HEADINGS:
                                     NG - Foreign Office
                                     NG - Political and racial
                                          Persecution

SUMMARY:

        Dossier contains copies of diplomatic notes exchanged
between the American charge d'affaires and the German Foreign
Office over German attempts to include American citizens of
Jewish faith in the provisions regarding the elimination of
Jews from the German economy (RGB. I, P. 414, 26 April 1938).

        Among the documents is a letter to RIBBENTROP, signed
by WEIZSAECKER, in which he refers to an enclosed draft of a
reply to the U.S. charge d'affaires, bearing WEIZSAECKER's
initials and pencil marks.

        In the cover letter to RIBBENTROP, WEIZSAECKER boasts
that the reply drafted by him is so clever, that the American
government can "hardly make political capital out of it against
us, nor, on the other hand, can they make much use of it".

        In the reply itself, WEIZSAECKER tells the American
government in effect that it is not authorized to prevent other
nations from applying discriminatory laws against her citizens.
Says he: "There is, however, no general principle of international law, which would obligate a state to refrain from applying
differential treatment for reasons of race or creed to foreign
citizens living within its borders". (P. Bоо5687)

Auswärtiges Amt

Büro St. S

Behandlung amerikanischer
Staatsbürger u. bezug auf
die Judengesetzgebung.

89

20.12.1938.

Schriftwechsel

zwischen der Amerikanischen Botschaft und dem Auswärtigen
Amt in Fragen der neueren Judengesetzgebung :

I.

Verordnung über die Anmeldung des Vermögens von
Juden vom 26. April 1938, RGBl.I S.414:

9.5.   Verbalnote der Amerikanischen Botschaft

17.5.   Zwischenbescheid des Auswärtigen Amts

24.6.   Antwort des Auswärtigen Amts durch Verbalnote.

25.6.   " Memorandum of Conversation" über eine Unterredung
mit V.L.R.Clodius wird im Auswärtigen Amt abgegeben.

30.6.   Verbalnote (Bestätigung der Antwort des Auswärtigen
Amts vom 24.6.) und erneute Mitteilung des amerikanischen
Standpunkts.

II.

Gelegentlich der Vorfälle am 8.,9. und 10.November
1938:

15.11.   Verbalnote der Amerikanischen Botschaft (persönlich
abgegeben)

III.

Verordnung zur Ausschliessung der Juden aus dem
deutschen Wirtschaftsleben vom 12.11.1938
RGBl.I S.1580 :

22.11.   Verbalnote der Amerikanischen Botschaft

10.12.   Antwort des Auswärtigen Amts durch Verbalnote.

IV.siehe unten

V.

Genereller Einspruch gegen die Ausdehnung der
deutschen Judengesetzgebung auf amerikanische Bürger

14.12.   Verbalnote des Amerikanischen ~~Botschaft~~ Geschäftsträger

20.12.   Verbalnote des Auswärtigen Amts (Zwischenbescheid)
~~befindet sich im Geschäftsgang.~~

IV.
Verordnung über den Einsatz des jüdischen V
vom 3.Dezember 1938 -RGBl.I S.170 :

8.12.   Note des Amerikanischen Geschäftsträgers.

- - - -

B 005664

Abschrift.

Berlin, May 9, 1938.

Excellency,

I have the honor to inform Your Excellency that I have
been instructed by my Government to bring the following
matter to the attention of the German Government.

On April 26, 1938, a decree was issued by the German
Government and supplemented by instructions under which
all Jews and their spouses whether German or foreign
nationals are called upon to declare, subject to certain
small exceptions, all property held in Germany while
such declarations are not required from Germans generally
nor from other foreigners. It appears further that the
Commissioner for the Four-Year-Plan is authorized to use
the fortunes so declared "in harmony with the requirements
of German economy."

The Government of the United States considers
that the application of measures of the nature indicated
to the property of American citizens of the Jewish race
would violate rights accorded American citizens under the
Treaty of Friendship, Commerce and Consular Rights between
the United States and Germany signed December 8, 1923.
Article I of this treaty in part provides:

"The nationals of each of the high contracting
parties shall be permitted to enter, travel and reside
in the territories of the other, to exercise liberty of
conscience and freedom of worship; to engage in professional, scientific, religious, philanthropic, manufacturing

and

91

B 005665/1

and commercial work of every kind without interference; to
carry on every form of commercial activity which is not
forbidden by the local law; to own, erect or lease and
occupy appropriate buildings and to lease lands for resi-
dential, scientific , religious, philanthropic, manufacturing, commercial and mortuary purposes; to employ agents
of their choice and generally to do anything incidental to
or necessary for the enjoyment of any of the foregoing
privileges upon the same terms as nationals of the state
of residence or as nationals of the nation hereafter to be
most favored by it, submitting themselves to all local laws
and regulations duly established.

92

"The nationals of each high contracting party shall
receive within the territories of the other, upon submitting
to the conditions imposed upon its nationals, the most
constant protection and security for their persons and proper
ty and shall enjoy in this respect that degree of protection
that is required by international law. Their property shall
not be taken without due process of law and without payment
of just compensation."

The foregoing provisions respecting rights in one
country are applicable to all the nationals of the other
country without exceptions based upon race or creed.

In view of the scope and purpose of the decree and
its discriminatory character, the Government of the United
States enters emphatic protest against its application
to American citizens. It feels that on further consideration of the matter, the German Government will agree with the

considera-

3

considerations set forth above and will give early assurances
that the measures will not be applied to American citizens.

In view of the urgency which this matter presents, the
Government of the United States would appreciate an early
reply from the German Government.

Accept, Excellency, the renewed assurance of my
highest consideration.

(sgd.) Hugh R.Wilson.

His Excellency Joachim von Ribbentrop, Minister for Foreign

Affairs , B e r l i n .

93

Abschrift/Angabe.

Auswärtiges Amt

82-32 9/5

Verbalnote.

Das Auswärtige Amt beehrt sich,der Botschaft der
Vereinigten Staaten von Amerika den Empfang der von dem Herrn
Amerikanischen Botschafter dem Herrn Reichsaußenminister
übergebenen Note Nr.69 vom 9.Mai d.J. betr. Anmeldung jüdischen Vermögens ergebenst zu bestätigen. Es hat nicht verfehlt, die zuständigen inneren Behörden mit der Angelegenheit zu befassen und darf sich weitere Nachricht ergebenst
vorbehalten.

Berlin, den 17. Mai 1938.

94

An die Botschaft der Vereinigten Staaten von Amerika.

Auswärtiges Amt
82 - 32 20/6.

NE-...

Verbalnote.

Das Auswärtige Amt beehrt sich, der Botschaft der
Vereinigten Staaten von Amerika auf die gefällige Verbalnote
vom 9.d.M. -Nr.69 - folgendes zu erwidern:

1.) Gemäß § 7 der Verordnung vom 26. April d.J. über die
Anmeldung des Vermögens von Juden sind Juden amerikanischer
Staatsangehörigkeit zur Anmeldung ihres in Deutschland
belegenen Vermögens verpflichtet. Das Auswärtige Amt darf
die Botschaft der Vereinigten Staaten von Amerika jedoch
davon in Kenntnis setzen, daß die zuständigen inneren Verwaltungsbehörden davon absehen werden, das Anmeldeverfahren
auf jüdisches Vermögen in der Hand von amerikanischen Staatsangehörigen durchzuführen, wenn diese ihren ständigen Wohnsitz im Ausland haben, es sei denn, daß es sich um emigrierte
frühere deutsche Reichsangehörige handelt.

2.) Falls gemäß § 7 der genannten Verordnung ein Einsatz
des registrierten jüdischen Vermögens im Rahmen der deutschen
Wirtschaft in Frage kommen sollte, darf das Auswärtige Amt
der Botschaft der Vereinigten Staaten von Amerika bereits
jetzt mitteilen, daß in jedem Einzelfall geprüft werden wird,
ob die in dem Deutsch-Amerikanischen Freundschafts-, Handels-
und Niederlassungsvertrag vom 8.Dezember 1923 gewährleisteten
Rechte amerikanischer Staatsangehöriger berücksichtigt sind.

Berlin, den 24. Juni 1938.

die Botschaft der Vereinigten Staaten von Amerika.

Abschrift 82 -32 25/6.

Memorandum of Conversation.

According to the Ministry for Foreign Affairs'
note No.82-32 20-6 of June 24, 1938, "the competent
internal administrative authorithies will waive application
of the registration procedure to Jewish property in the
hands of American nationals if the latter have their
permanent domicile abroad, unless they are former Reich
nationals who have emigrated."

The Embassy of the United States of America under-
stands, however, from the information furnished orally
yesterday by Dr.Clodius, that in practice registration
will be required only of the property of those former
Reich nationals who have emigrated for political reasons
since 1933. Jewish property in the hands of American nationals who are former Reich nationals but who emigrated prior
to 1933, or if their emigration occurred subsequent to that
date are not considered as having emigrated for political
reasons, will not be subject to the registration procedure
under the provisions of Article 7 of the Decree of April 26,
1938.

American Embassy,

Berlin, June 25, 1938.

DRH:AC

Abschrift 82 - 32 30/6.
Embassy of the United States of America
No.136

The Embassy of the United States of America has
the honor to acknowledge the receipt of the note of the
Ministry for Foreign Affairs of June 24, 1938 (No.82-32
20-6), in which it is stated that the German Government
will waive application of the registration procedure prescribed under the Decree of April 26, 1938, to Jewish property
in the hands of American nationals if the latter have their
permanent domicile abroad, unless they are former Reich
nationals who have emigrated. The Embassy also refers to oral
assurances received at the Ministry for Foreign Affairs
that in the execution of this decree the German Government
will also not require the registration of Jewish property
of American citizens resident outside of Germany but formerly of German nationality, provided they had not emigrated
from Germany since 1933 for political reasons.

According to the note under acknowledgment as
supplemented by the oral assurances above referred to,
Jewish property in the hands of American citizens resident
in Germany, as well as such property of American citizens
who emigrated from Germany for political reasons since 1933,
will still be subject to the provisions of the decree in
question. Since therefore there will still remain discrimination against American citizens, the Embassy is instructed
again to record the firm position of the Government of the
United States, in accordance with the provisions of the

Treaty

97

Treaty of Friendship, Commerce, and Consular Rights
of December 8, 1923, that the rights of American citizens
in Germany should receive full protection without exception
based upon race or creed.

Berlin, June 30, 1938

To the Ministry for Foreign Affairs , Berlin

- - - - - - - -

98

The Embassy of the United States of America

No.240

The Embassy of the United States of America
has the honor to inform the Ministry for Foreign Affairs
that the Embassy has been advised of damage to certain
American business properties in Germany which occurred
in the course of the recent anti-Jewish manifestations
and to state that on behalf of American owners of such
properties the Government of the United States of America
reserves all rights.

Berlin, November 15, 1938.

99

To

the Ministry for Foreign Affairs,
              B e r l i n .

The Embassy of the United States of America
No.244

The Embassy of the United States of America has the
honor to refer to a decree of the German Government, dated
November 12, 1938, which was published in the Reichsgesetzblatt, Part I, No.189, of November 14, 1938 providing for
the elimination of Jews (as defined in Section 5 of the
First Decree to the Reich Citizenship Law of November 14,
1938) from various commercial activities. It is also noted
that Jewish undertakings (as defined in the Third Decree
to the Reich Citizenship Law of June 13, 1938) which are
carried on in contravention of this prohibition are to be
closed by the Police.

100

The Embassy has found no provision in this decree
which would exempt American citizens from its stipulations.
It notes, however, that the issuance of executory regulations
are authorized and assumes that such will be issued in due
course.

In an interview granted by the German Minister for
Propaganda and Public Enlightenment to a correspondent
of the Reuter Agency on November 12, in effect simultan-
eous with the issuance of the decree in question, and
published in the Berlin press on November 15th, the Minister
is quoted as having stated that the pertinent decrees of
November 12, 1938 would not apply to Jews of other nationalities. The Embassy of the United States, in view of the high
authority as Minister of the German Reich by whom the

statement

B 005673

statemant cited was enunciated, feels that it can enjoy
full confidence that the decree in question is not applicable
to American citizens. It would, however, in order that
in its relations with various authorities of the German
Government it may in its affairs possess an understanding
necessary to their proper conduct, appreciate an early
assurance from the Ministry of Foreign Affairs that the
interpretation of the application of this decree is as has just
been stated.

Berlin, November 22, 1938

P.B.C.

101

Abschrift Angabe
Auswärtiges Amt
84 - 60 3/12 Sdh Ang.I

Verbalnote.

Das Auswärtige Amt beehrt sich der Botschaft der
Vereinigten Staaten auf die gefällige Verbalnote vom 22.
v.M. -No.244- und im Anschluß an die Verbalnote des Auswärtigen Amts vom 29.v.M. -84-60 22/11 - folgendes zu erwidern:

Gemäß der Verordnung zur Ausschaltung der Juden aus
der deutschen Wirtschaft vom 12. November 1938, ist allen
Juden vom 1.Januar 1939 ab der Betrieb von Einzelhandels-
verkaufsstellen, Versandgeschäften oder Bestellkontoren
sowie der selbständige Betrieb eines Handwerks untersagt.
Ferner ist ihnen mit Wirkung vom gleichen Tage verboten,
auf Märkten aller Art Messen oder Ausstellungen Waren
oder gewerbliche Leistungen anzubieten, dafür zu werben
oder Bestellungen darauf anzunehmen.

Diese Verordnung bezieht sich auch auf Juden, die
eine ausländische Staatsangehörigkeit besitzen. Die zuständigen inneren Verwaltungsbehörden werden aber vor Er-
greifung von Maßnahmen in allen Fällen, in denen es sich um
amerikanische Bürger handelt, die Bestimmungen der in Gel-
tung befindlichen deutsch-amerikanischen Vereinbarungen
berücksichtigen.

Das Auswärtige Amt darf sich hierbei auf die Ausführungen in seiner Verbalnote vom 24.Juni d.J.- 82-32 20/6.-
beziehen.   Berlin,den 10.Dezember 1938
An die Botschaft der Vereinigten Staaten von Amerika.

No. 260.

Excellency:

I have the honour to bring the following to the attention of Your Excellency.

By a German decree of December 3, 1938, respecting the employment of Jewish capital, which was published in the Reichsgesetzblatt I, No. 206, of December 5, 1938, it appears that the owner (Inhaber) of Jewish industrial undertakings (as defined in the Third Decree of June 14, 1938, to the Reich Citizen Law) can be instructed under Article I to sell or to liquidate such undertakings according to conditions stipulated in the decree. Under Article II of the same decree, it appears that Jewish owners of real property can likewise be instructed to sell such property, and persones of the Jewish race are furthermore legally forbidden to acquire real property or rights pertaining thereto. I have taken note that Article I and Article II of the decree cited, which relate to the questions briefly summarized above, do not by their terms exempt American citizens from their application.

In view of the stipulation of Article I of the Treaty of Friendship, Commerce and Consular Rights between the United States and Germany of December 8, 1923, I am confident that, in the application of this decree, the property of American citizens will be exempted from its provisions in those articles wherein exemption is not specifically provided for Jews of foreign

nationalities

103

nationalities, and I should appreciate the early
assurances of Your Excellency to this effect.

Accept, Excellency, the renewed assurance
of my highest consideration.

Prentiss Gilbert

Chargé d'Affaires ad interim

Berlin, December 8, 1938.

His Excellency

Joachim von Ribbentrop,

Minister of Foreign Affairs,

B e r l i n .

104

Abschrift   84-60 Sdh.14/12.

No.263

Excellency :

I have been instructed by my Government to express its
disappointment that Your Excellency's Government has not as
yet conveyed the assurances which my Government felt confident
would be received concerning non-discriminatory treatment in
Germany of American citizens without exception based on race
or creed.

The attention of Your Excellency's Government was ex-
pressly invited to this matter in Mr.Wilson's note of May 9,
1938,and my Government's concern and its desire for the assurances sought therein have been reiterated on several occa-
sions in communications to Your Excellency's Government.

My Government is concerned with the provisions of the
decree laws which if made applicable to American citizens
would have the effect of arbitrarily dividing them into special
classes and subject them to differential treatment on the
basis of such classification.It is one of the fundamental
principles of my Government to make no distinction between
American citizens on the basis of race or creed,and uniformly
in its relations with foreign nations it has emphatically de-
clined the right of those nations to apply on their part
such discrimination as between American citizens. This principle furthermore is applied by my Government to nationals
of foreign countries residing in the United States,including
Germans. The application to American citizens of the measures
referred to would be incompatible with this principle.

My Government believes,therefore,that upon further consideration Your Excellency's Government will decide that American
                                                    citizens

His Excellency
Joachim von Ribbentrop,
    Minister for Foreign Affairs
        B e r l i n.

105

citizens will not be discriminated against in Germany on account of race or creed and that they will not be subjected to provisions of the nature of those embodied in the decree laws in question.

Accept, Excellency, the renewed assurance of my highest consideration .

(s) Prentiss Gilbert
Chargé d'Affaires ad interim.

Berlin, December 14, 1938.

106

TELEGRAMM
aus Washington vom 16.Dezember 1938.

Zu der Vorgeschichte und den Gründen,welche die Ab-
sendung der gestrigen amerikanischen Note veranlaßten,habe
ich inzwischen folgendes zuverlässig in Erfahrung gebracht:

Wie bereits angenommen wurde, stammt der Entwurf zu
der ..... +) vom Präsidenten selbst.Der Präsident verfolgt
mit ihr die Absicht,eine klare Entscheidung über die künf-
tigen Beziehungen zu Deutschland herbeizuführen.Werde die
Note von Deutschland in befriedigendem Sinne beantwortet,
so werde dies wahrscheinlich als hinreichend angesehen werden,um Botschafter Wilson nach Berlin zurückzusenden.Falls
die Reichsregierung ihm,dem Präsidenten,aber hierzu die
Hand nicht biete,so müsse die Amerikanische Regierung die
Verhängung von Gegenmaßnahmen ernstlich in Erwägung ziehen.

In State Department wird zugegeben,daß alle amerikanische Juden betreffenden Einzelfälle zufriedenstellende
Erledigung gefunden hätten.Es handelte sich jetzt aber da-
rum,daß die Reichsregierung die unzweideutige Versicherung
abgebe,daß sie auch in Zukunft gegen amerikanische Staatsangehörige in Deutschland keine Maßnahmen ergreifen werde,die
auf "race or creed" beruhen. Erst unter dieser Voraussetzung
könnten die Beziehungen zwischen Deutschland und Amerika
wieder normalisiert werden.Bei dieser Initiative Roosevelts
ist zu berücksichtigen,daß die Amerikanische Regierung
bestrebt ist,durch scharfe Sprache gegenüber Deutschland
die öffentliche Meinung von anderen außenpolitischen Miß-
erfolgen abzulenken(offene Tür-Politik Lima).Andererseits
wird Regierung sich allmählich davon überzeugt haben,

                                                    Bogen

fehlt
1"Note"

B 005680

Bogen gegenüber Deutschland überspannt zu haben und sie
sucht daher nach einem Weg,unter Wahrung ihres Prestiges
normale Beziehungen durch Rücksendung Wilsons wiederherzu-
stellen.Dieses Ziel glaubt sie erreichen zu können,wenn
sie hiesiger Öffentlichkeit entgegenkommende deutsche Er-
klärung präsentieren kann.Der auf die Regierung ausgeübte
Druck zahlreicher Boykottorganisationen mit dem Ziel Verhängung wirtschaftlicher Gegenmaßnahmen gegen Deutschland
ist nach wie vor äusserst stark.Man erkennt deutlich,daß
die Regierung in dieser Situation zu lavieren versucht;
immerhin wird mit Entschlossenheit des Präsidenten gerechnet
werden müssen,die alternativen Wirtschaftsgegenmaßnahmen
zu ergreifen.

gez.Thomsen.

108

Abschrift 84-60.17/12.Sdhft.

TELEGRAMM
aus Washington vom 17.Dezember 1938.

Neue vertrauliche Informationen und Haltung amerikanischer Presse zur Veröffentlichung letzter amerikanischer Note in Judenfrage verstärkt Eindruck, daß unsere Beziehungen zu Vereinigten Staaten in entscheidender Phase stehen. Präsident steht unter stärkstem Druck der radikalen und jüdischen Kreise,die im Hinblick auf deutsche Maßnahmen gegen Juden,ferner angeblich auch im Hinblick auf die Rechte und Interessen amerikanischer Bürger jüdischer Rasse sowie diskriminierende Maßnahmen gegen amerikanischen Handel Repressalien gegen Deutschland verlangten.Hierbei wird vor allem Zollerhöhung auf deutsche Waren um fünfzig vom Hundert auf Grund der dem Präsidenten nach Sektion 338 Zolltarifgesetzes zustehenden Befugnisse angestrebt.

109

Auf der anderen Seite sind nach zuverlässigen Nachrichten auch starke Kräfte am Werke,die sich bemühen,auf den Präsidenten im Sinne einer Normalisierung der Beziehungen zwischen beiden Ländern einzuwirken.

Mit letzter Note will Präsident offensichtlich eine Entscheidung in der einen oder anderen Richtung herbeiführen. Nach vorliegenden Nachrichten muß man annehmen, daß der Präsident bei Ausbleiben der gewünschten Zusicherung von Anwendung der von ihm geforderten Gegenmaßnahmen nicht zurückschrecken wird,und daß damit das Judentum sein Ziel erreicht.

Lage darstellt sich demnach zur Zeit so,daß durch eine Bestätigung der in letzter Note vertretenen amerikanischen Auffassung durch uns eine Normalisierung der Beziehungen erreichbar erscheint.Diese Normalisierung würde aber wohl nur erreicht werden können,wenn amerikanischer Regierung

gestattet

gestattet werden würde,die deutsche Antwortnote zu veröffentlichen,denn sie braucht für die hiesige Öffentlichkeit
einen nach außen sichtbaren Anlaß,um Botschafter Wilson
wieder nach Berlin zurücksenden zu können.Aus der Be -
schränkung der letzten amerikanischen Note auf die Frage
der Behandlung amerikanischer Bürger jüdischer Rasse in
Deutschland ergibt sich, daß man amerikanischerseits <u>in
diesem Zusammenhang</u> Zusicherungen auf die bekannten 6 Be-
schwerdepunkte (vgl.Aufzeichnung Botschafters Dieckhoff
vom 28.7.d.J.)nicht verlangt.Offenbar hat die sachliche
und ruhige Berichterstattung Wilsons wesentlich dazu beigetragen,daß Präsident seine anmaßende Stellungnahme zur
deutschen Judenfrage zurückgesteckt hat und sich heute
auf amerikanische Interessen und Erwägungen beschränkt.

gez.Thomsen.

110

Berlin, den   Dezember 1938.   zu 84-60, Sdh.14/12.

An
                                        St.S.
                                        R.M.
den Geschäftsträger der Vereinigten
Staaten von Amerika   Sofort
Herrn Prentiss B.Gilbert.

                              Herr Geschäftsträger !

                                        Auf Ihre Note vom 14.
                              Dezember d.J.- No.263- über die Behandlung
                              amerikanischer Bürger in Deutschland beehre
                              ich mich Ihnen Folgendes zu erwidern:

                                        Nach Ihrer Note hält sich die
                              Regierung der Vereinigten Staaten von Amerika
                              für berechtigt, von der Deutschen Regierung
                              eine allgemeine Zusicherung des Inhalts zu
Bei   fordern, dass amerikanische Bürger in
Dir.X   Deutschland wegen ihrer Rasse oder ihres
Dir.V.   Glaubens keiner unterschiedlichen Behandlung
                              unterworfen werden sollen. Sie meint diese
Pol..IX   Forderung auf die Behauptung stützen zu   111
                              können, dass es einer ihrer fundamentalen
zur Kitz.   Grundsätze sei, keine Unterschiede zwischen
                              amerikanischen Bürgern auf Grund von Rasse
                              und Glauben zu machen, und dass sie in
                              ihren Beziehungen zu anderen Staaten diesen
                              stets das Recht bestritten habe, ihrerseits
                                                 solche

solche Unterscheidung auf amerikanische

Bürger anzuwenden.

Es ist selbstverständlich das Recht

der Regierung der Vereinigten Staaten von

Amerika, wie jeder souveränen Regierung,

in den hier in Betracht kommenden Fragen

für die von ihr im eigenen Lande zu treffen-

den Massnahmen politische Grundsätze dieser

oder jener Art aufzustellen. ~~Es ist aber~~

~~offensichtlich eine~~ ganz andere Frage, ob

solche Grundsätze auch für andere Regierungen

hinsichtlich der in deren ~~Gast~~ Hoheitsbereich

fallenden Massnahmen verbindliche Kraft

besitzen. ~~Das ist~~ nur dann der Fall, wenn

derartige Grundsätze entweder allgemein

anerkannten Regeln des Völkerrechts ent-

sprächen oder wenn sie zwischen einzelnen

Staaten zum Gegenstand besonderer Verein-

barungen gemacht worden ~~sind.~~ wäre.

~~Ein~~ allgemeiner Grundsatz des

Völkerrechts, ~~der keinen~~ Staat verpflichtet,

von ~~jeder~~ unterschiedlichen Behandlung

der in seinem Lande lebenden fremden

Staatsangehörigen nach Rasse oder Glauben

oder anderen Merkmalen abzusehen, ~~besteht~~

~~nicht.~~ Die Deutsche Regierung ist auch

nicht

112

B 005685

nicht die erste und nicht die einzige,
die eine solche unterschiedliche Behandlung
in gewissen Fragen für notwendig erachtet
hat. Sie hat dies aber in keinem Falle
etwa auf Grund der fremden Staatsangehörigkeit der betroffenen Personen getan, sondern
besondere Massnahmen der in Rede stehenden
Art auf bestimmte Kategorien fremder Staatsangehöriger nur dann zur Anwendung gebracht,
wenn auch die eigenen Staatsangehörigen der
gleichen Kategorien diesen Massnahmen unterworfen wurden. Darüber hinaus hat die Deutsch
Regierung in dieser Beziehung fremden Staatsangehörigen in allen denjenigen Punkten,
wo sich die sachlich nur irgendwie als
möglich erwies, sogar gesetzlich eine
günstigere Behandlung als den eigenen
Staatsangehörigen zugestanden.

Es bleibt mithin nur die Frage übrig,
ob und inwieweit etwa besondere vertragliche
Abmachungen zwischen Deutschland und den
Vereinigten Staaten von Amerika der Anwendung der von der Amerikanischen Regierung
beanstandeten deutschen Massnahmen auf
amerikanische Bürger entgegenstehen. In
dieser Hinsicht hat das Auswärtige Amt

der

113

der Amerikanischen Botschaft schon wieder holt
mündlich und schriftlich erklärt, dass die
Deutsche Regierung selbstverständlich die
den amerikanischen Bürgern auf Grund von
Staatsverträgen zustehenden Rechte respektieren werde. Die Amerikanische Botschaft
hat dem Auswärtigen Amt bisher keinen Einzelfall mitgeteilt, in dem nach ihrer Ansicht solche vertraglichen Rechte durch
deutsche Massnahmen verletzt worden wären.
Die Deutsche Regierung ist ~~aber noch wie~~
~~vor~~ bereit, wenn ihr solche Fälle von der
Amerikanischen Botschaft mitgeteilt werden
sollten, sie an Hand der geltenden Ver-
tragsbestimmungen sorgsam zu prüfen und
zu regeln.

Genehmigen Sie, Herr Geschäftsträger,
die Versicherung meiner vorzüglichsten
Hochachtung.

(I.R.. gez.
.....)

114

Berlin, den 27. Dezember 1938.

Dem Herrn Reichsminister.

Auf die bekannte amerikanische Note vom
14. ds. Mts., betreffend die Behandlung amerikanischer
Juden in Deutschland ist im Auswärtigen Amt der anlie-
gende Noten-Entwurf verfaßt worden.

Der Gedanke, welcher dem Entwurf zu Grunde
liegt, ist, den Vereinigten Staaten und zwar vor der Er-
öffnung des Kongresses am 3. Januar eine Antwort zu erteilen, aus welcher die Amerikanische Regierung schwerlich
Kapital gegen uns schlagen, andererseits aber auch nicht
viel Nutzen ziehen kann.

Es ist beabsichtigt, am 29. ds. Mts. den
beteiligten inneren Stellen, jedenfalls dem Reichswirtschaft
schaftsministerium Kenntnis von der Art und Weise zu geben, wie wir antworten wollen und dann die Note noch vor
Jahresschluß der hiesigen Amerikanischen Botschaft auszu-
händigen.

Ich wäre dankbar für Zustimmung zu dem
beschriebenen Vorgehen.

B 005692

Berlin, den 27. Dezember 1938.

- 84-60 Sch. 14/12 -

Herr Geschäftsträger!

     Auf Ihre Note vom 14. Dezember ds.Js. -
Nr. 263 - über die Behandlung amerikanischer Bürger in
Deutschland beehre ich mich Ihnen Folgendes zu erwidern:

     Nach Ihrer Note ~~hält sich~~ die Regierung
der Vereinigten Staaten von ~~Amerika~~ ~~für berechtigt~~, von
der Deutschen Regierung eine allgemeine Zusicherung des
Inhalts ~~zu fordern~~, daß amerikanische Bürger in Deutschland wegen ihrer Rasse oder ihres Glaubensbekenntnisses
keiner unterschiedlichen Behandlung unterworfen werden ~~sol-
len~~. ~~Sie meint~~ diese ~~Forderung~~ auf die Behauptung stützen
zu können, daß es einer ihrer fundamentalen Grundsätze sei,
keine Unterschiede zwischen amerikanischen Bürgern auf
Grund von Rasse und Glaubensbekenntnis zu machen und daß
sie in ihren Beziehungen zu anderen Staaten diesen stets
das Recht bestritten habe, ihrerseits solche Unterscheidung auf amerikanische Bürger anzuwenden.

                                Es

116

An den
   Geschäftsträger der Vereinigten
   Staaten von Amerika
     Herrn Prentiss B. Gilbert,
       <u>Berlin.</u>

Es ist selbstverständlich das Recht der
Regierung der Vereinigten Staaten von Amerika, wie
jeder souveränen Regierung, in den hier in Betracht
kommenden Fragen für die von ihr im eigenen Lande
zu treffenden Maßnahmen politische Grundsätze dieser
oder jener Art aufzustellen. Eine ganz andere Frage
ist es aber, ob solche Grundsätze auch für andere
Regierungen hinsichtlich der in deren Hoheitsbereich
fallenden Maßnahmen verbindliche Kraft besitzen. Of-
fenbar wäre das nur dann der Fall, wenn derartige
Grundsätze entweder allgemein anerkannten Regeln des
Völkerrechts entsprächen oder wenn sie zwischen einzelnen Staaten zum Gegenstand besonderer Vereinbarungen gemacht worden wären.

117

Es besteht jedoch kein allgemeiner Grundsatz
des Völkerrechts, wonach ein Staat verpflichtet wäre,
von unterschiedlicher Behandlung der in seinem Lande
lebenden fremden Staatsangehörigen nach Rasse oder
Glauben oder anderen Merkmalen abzusehen. Die Deutsche
Regierung ist auch nicht die erste und nicht die einzige, die eine solche unterschiedliche Behandlung in
gewissen Fragen für notwendig erachtet hat. Sie hat dies
aber in keinem Falle etwa auf Grund der fremden Staatsangehörigkeit der betroffenen Personen getan, sondern
besondere Maßnahmen der in Rede stehenden Art auf bestimmte

B 005694

stimmte Kategorien fremder Staatsangehöriger nur dann zur
Anwendung gebracht, wenn auch die eigenen Staatsangehörigen der gleichen Kategorien diesen Maßnahmen unterworfen
wurden. Darüber hinaus hat die Deutsche Regierung in dieser Beziehung aus besonderem Entgegenkommen fremden Staatsangehörigen da, wo es sich sachlich als angängig erwies,
sogar gesetzlich eine günstigere Behandlung als den eigenen Staatsangehörigen zugestanden.

Es bleibt mithin nur die Frage übrig, ob und inwieweit etwa besondere vertragliche Abmachungen zwischen
Deutschland und den Vereinigten Staaten von Amerika der
Anwendung der von der Amerikanischen Regierung beanstandeten deutschen Maßnahmen auf amerikanische Bürger entgegenstehen. In dieser Hinsicht hat das Auswärtige Amt der Amerikanischen Botschaft schon wiederholt mündlich und schriftlich erklärt, daß die Deutsche Regierung selbstverständlich die den amerikanischen Bürgern auf Grund von Staatsverträgen zustehenden Rechte respektieren werde. Die Amerikanische Botschaft hat dem Auswärtigen Amt bisher keinen
Einzelfall mitgeteilt, in dem nach ihrer Ansicht solche
vertraglichen Rechte durch deutsche Maßnahmen verletzt
worden wären. Die Deutsche Regierung ist im übrigen bereit,
wenn ihr solche Fälle von der Amerikanischen Botschaft
mitgeteilt werden sollten, sie an Hand der geltenden Ver-
tragsbestimmungen zu prüfen und zu regeln.

                                        Genehmigen

Genehmigen Sie, Herr Geschäftsträger,
die Versicherung meiner vorzüglichsten Hochachtung.

119

Reichsgesetzblatt

Teil I

1938	Ausgegeben zu Berlin, den 23. Mai 1938	Nr. 83

Verordnung über die Arbeitszeit der Beamten*).

Vom 13. Mai 1938.

Auf Grund des § 16 Abs. 1 des Deutschen Beamtengesetzes vom 26. Januar 1937 (Reichsgesetzbl. I S. 39) wird hierdurch verordnet:

Doc. 11

120

§ 1

(1) Die Arbeitszeit der Beamten beträgt wöchentlich 51 Stunden, in den Städten Berlin, Hamburg, München, Köln und Dresden 48½ Stunden, sofern dort nicht geteilte Arbeitszeit zugelassen wird (vgl. jedoch § 11).

(2) Soweit der Dienst in Bereitschaft besteht, ist die Dienstzeit entsprechend den Bedürfnissen der Verwaltung zu erhöhen.

(3) Der Beamte ist verpflichtet, ohne Entschädigung auch über die regelmäßige Arbeitszeit hinaus Dienst zu tun, wenn die dienstlichen Verhältnisse es fordern. Zum Ausgleich einer außergewöhnlichen dienstlichen Mehrbeanspruchung eines Beamten außerhalb der Dienststunden kann der Dienststellenleiter ihm Dienstbefreiung zu anderer Zeit gewähren.

§ 2

Die Tagesarbeitszeit ist grundsätzlich in Vor- und Nachmittagsdienst zu teilen.

§ 3

In Städten mit mehr als 500 000 Einwohnern bildet die durchgehende Arbeitszeit die Regel. Auf Antrag des Reichsstatthalters — in Preußen des Oberpräsidenten — kann der Reichsminister des Innern geteilte Arbeitszeit zulassen.

§ 4

Für Städte mit mehr als 100 000 Einwohnern, in denen eine Teilung der Arbeitszeit in Vor- und Nachmittagsdienst infolge der örtlichen Verhältnisse zu erheblichen Unzuträglichkeiten führen würde, kann auf Antrag des Reichsstatthalters — in Preußen des Oberpräsidenten — vom Reichsminister des Innern im Benehmen mit dem Reichsminister der Finanzen durchgehende Arbeitszeit festgesetzt werden. Dieselbe Anordnung kann für Städte mit weniger als 100 000 Einwohnern jeweils vorübergehend getroffen werden, wenn ein erheblicher Teil der Beamten wegen Wohnungsmangels außerhalb des Dienstortes wohnen muß; die Anordnung kann auf einzelne Behörden beschränkt werden.

§ 5

Allgemein ist anzustreben, daß der Dienstbeginn bei allen Dienststellen an demselben Orte gleichmäßig festgesetzt wird. Der Dienst soll in der Zeit vom 1. März bis Ende Oktober nicht vor 7 Uhr, in Städten mit durchgehender Arbeitszeit nicht vor 7½ Uhr, in der Zeit vom 1. November bis Ende Februar allgemein nicht vor 7½ Uhr beginnen. Der Dienst soll an keinem Tage vor 13 Uhr enden.

§ 6

In Städten mit durchgehender Arbeitszeit ist der Sonnabendnachmittag dienstfrei zu halten; jedoch darf der Dienst an den übrigen 5 Wochentagen 9 Stunden nicht übersteigen. In Orten mit geteilter Tagesarbeitszeit ist Mittwoch und Sonnabend durchgehend zu arbeiten und der Nachmittag dienstfrei zu halten; die regelmäßige Arbeitszeit darf an den übrigen 4 Wochentagen 9 Stunden nicht übersteigen.

*) Betrifft nicht das Land Österreich.

§ 7

An den Tagen vor Weihnachten, Neujahr, Pfingsten und am 20. April endet der Dienst um 13 Uhr. Der Tag vor Ostern ist dienstfrei. Für andere Tage darf Dienstfreiheit nur von den obersten Reichsbehörden im Benehmen mit dem Reichsminister des Innern, in Ausnahmefällen, die durch rein örtliche Gründe bedingt sind, in Landkreisen auch vom Landrat mit Ermächtigung des Regierungspräsidenten, in Stadtkreisen vom Regierungspräsidenten und, wenn der Anlaß nur eine einzelne Verwaltung berührt, vom Leiter dieser Verwaltung angeordnet werden. An die Stelle des Landrats und des Regierungspräsidenten treten in den außerpreußischen Ländern die Leiter der den Landratsämtern und den Regierungen entsprechenden Behörden der allgemeinen und inneren Verwaltung.

§ 8

Die obersten Dienstbehörden regeln im Rahmen des § 1 Abs. 2, inwieweit bei bestimmten Dienststellen und Verwaltungszweigen ihres Geschäftsbereichs Sonder- oder Sonntagsdienst einzurichten ist. Der Sonderdienst an den im § 7 genannten Tagen soll nicht länger als bis 17 Uhr dauern.

§ 9

Der Dienst ist in der Regel an der Dienststelle und innerhalb der vorgeschriebenen Tagesarbeitszeit zu leisten. Dem Dienst an der Dienststelle ist die Teilnahme an Sitzungen, Besichtigungen und dergleichen gleichzuachten. Soweit die Erledigung des Dienstes an der Dienststelle oder innerhalb der vorgeschriebenen Tagesarbeitszeit aus dienstlichen Gründen unzweckmäßig ist, kann der Dienststellenleiter den Dienst anderweitig regeln.

Berlin, den 13. Mai 1938.

Der Reichsminister des Innern
Frick

Der Reichsminister der Finanzen
In Vertretung
Reinhardt

§ 10

Die Bestimmungen dieser Verordnung gelten nur für die hauptamtlich tätigen Beamten. Die Arbeitszeit der übrigen Beamten ist gegebenenfalls nach Bedürfnis zu regeln.

§ 11

Die Arbeitszeit der Betriebsverwaltungen wird, soweit es sich nicht um die eigentliche Verwaltung handelt, durch die obersten Dienstbehörden besonders geregelt. Dasselbe gilt für die Deutsche Reichsbahn, die Deutsche Reichspost und die Reichsbank sowie für Anstalten, Einrichtungen und sonstige Dienststellen, deren Eigenart es erfordert.

§ 12

Die §§ 1 bis 11 sind auch für die Beamten der Gemeinden, Gemeindeverbände sowie sonstigen Körperschaften, Anstalten und Stiftungen des öffentlichen Rechts verbindlich.

§ 13

Für den Dienst der Leiter und Lehrer an öffentlichen Schulen und Hochschulen erläßt der Reichsminister für Wissenschaft, Erziehung und Volksbildung, für die Wehrmachtbeamten das Oberkommando der Wehrmacht, für die Richter der Reichsminister der Justiz und für die Beamten der Vollzugspolizei der Reichsführer ⚡⚡ und Chef der Deutschen Polizei im Reichsministerium des Innern besondere Anordnungen.

§ 14

Diese Verordnung tritt mit Wirkung vom 1. Juli 1938 in Kraft.

121

Verordnung über die Einführung der Nürnberger Rassengesetze im Lande Österreich.
Vom 20. Mai 1938.

Auf Grund des Artikels II des Gesetzes über die Wiedervereinigung Österreichs mit dem Deutschen Reich vom 13. März 1938 (Reichsgesetzbl. I S. 237) wird folgendes verordnet:

Artikel I

Reichsbürgergesetz

§ 1

Im Lande Österreich gelten

1. das Reichsbürgergesetz vom 15. September 1935 (Reichsgesetzbl. I S. 1146),

2. § 2 Abs. 2, § 4 Abs. 1, 3 und 4, §§ 5, 6 Abs. 1 sowie § 7 der Ersten Verordnung zum Reichsbürgergesetz vom 14. November 1935 (Reichsgesetzbl. I S. 1333).

§ 2

Den Zeitpunkt des Inkrafttretens des § 1 Abs. 2 des Reichsbürgergesetzes bestimmt der Reichsminister des Innern.

§ 3

Das Ausscheiden der Juden aus den öffentlichen Ämtern, die sie beim Inkrafttreten dieser Verordnung bekleiden, wird besonders geregelt.

§ 4

Für die Anwendung des § 5 Abs. 2 der Ersten Verordnung zum Reichsbürgergesetz ist auch im Lande Österreich als Tag des Erlasses des Reichsbürgergesetzes der 16. September 1935 und als Tag des Inkrafttretens des Gesetzes zum Schutze des deutschen Blutes und der deutschen Ehre der 17. September 1935 anzusehen.

Artikel II
Blutschutzgesetz

§ 5

Im Lande Österreich gelten das Gesetz zum Schutze des deutschen Blutes und der deutschen Ehre vom 15. September 1935 (Reichsgesetzbl. I S. 1146) und die Erste Verordnung zur Ausführung dieses Gesetzes vom 14. November 1935 (Reichsgesetzbl. I S. 1334).

§ 6

§ 3 des Blutschutzgesetzes tritt erst am 1. August 1938 in Kraft.

§ 7

Für die Anwendung des § 12 Abs. 3 der Ersten Ausführungsverordnung zum Blutschutzgesetz ist auch im Lande Österreich als Tag des Erlasses des Blutschutzgesetzes der 16. September 1935 anzusehen.

§ 8

(1) Eine Ehe darf nicht geschlossen werden, bevor nicht durch ein Zeugnis des für den ordentlichen Wohnsitz der Braut örtlich zuständigen Bürgermeisters nachgewiesen wird, daß ein Ehehindernis nach den Bestimmungen des Blutschutzgesetzes und der Ersten Ausführungsverordnung zu diesem Gesetz nicht besteht. Hat die Braut keinen ordentlichen Wohnsitz im Lande Österreich, so richtet sich die Zuständigkeit des Bürgermeisters nach den weiteren Bestimmungen des § 3 des Allgemeinen Verwaltungsverfahrensgesetzes (Österr. BGBl. Nr. 274/1925).

(2) Hat der Bürgermeister Zweifel, ob ein Ehehindernis im Sinne des § 6 der Ersten Ausführungsverordnung zum Blutschutzgesetz vorliegt, so hat er von den Brautleuten die Beibringung eines Ehetauglichkeitszeugnisses des Amtsarztes zu verlangen.

§ 9

Für die Anwendung des § 15 Satz 2 der Ersten Ausführungsverordnung zum Blutschutzgesetz steht der frühere Besitz der österreichischen Bundesbürgerschaft dem früheren Besitz der deutschen Staatsangehörigkeit gleich.

Artikel III
Verfahrensvorschriften

§ 10

Auf die Nichtigkeitsklage finden die Vorschriften des österreichischen Rechts über die Zuständigkeit und das Verfahren der Gerichte in Rechtsstreitigkeiten über die Ungültigerklärung der Ehe sinngemäß mit folgender Maßgabe Anwendung:

1. Die Klage ist gegen beide Ehegatten zu richten. Legt der Staatsanwalt oder einer der Ehegatten ein Rechtsmittel ein, so sind im ersten Fall beide Ehegatten, im zweiten der Staatsanwalt und der andere Ehegatte als Gegner anzusehen.

2. Die Vorschriften über den Anwaltszwang finden auf den Staatsanwalt keine Anwendung.

3. Unterliegt der Staatsanwalt, so ist die Staatskasse zur Erstattung der den Ehegatten erwachsenden Kosten nach Maßgabe der §§ 40 ff. der österreichischen Zivilprozeßordnung zu verurteilen.

4. Ein Ehebandsverteidiger wird nicht bestellt.

5. Die Klage kann nur zu Lebzeiten beider Ehegatten erhoben werden. Stirbt einer der Ehegatten vor der Rechtskraft des Urteils, so ist der Rechtsstreit als in der Hauptsache erledigt anzusehen.

§ 11

Für Zuwiderhandlungen gegen § 5 Abs. 1 und 2 des Blutschutzgesetzes ist der Gerichtshof erster Instanz zuständig.

Artikel IV
Schlußvorschriften

§ 12

Soweit Vorschriften, die durch diese Verordnung im Lande Österreich eingeführt werden, nicht unmittelbar angewandt werden können, sind sie sinngemäß anzuwenden.

§ 13

Diese Verordnung tritt am Tage nach der Verkündung in Kraft.

Berlin, den 20. Mai 1938.

Der Reichsminister des Innern

Frick

Der Stellvertreter des Führers

R. Heß

Der Reichsminister der Justiz

In Vertretung

Dr. Schlegelberger

Translation
from
REICHSGESETZBLATT Part I, No. 83, May 23, 1938.

Decree governing the
introduction of the Nuremberg
Racial Laws in the Province
of Austria. Of May 20, 1938.

———————

. On the basis of Article II of the Law of March 13,
1938, governing the Reunion of Austria with the German
Reich (REICHSGESETZBLATT I page 237), the following is
decreed:

Article I

Reich Citizens Law

Section 1.

The following apply in the Province of Austria:

1. The Reich Citizens Law of September 15, 1935
    (REICHSGESETZBLATT I page 1146),

2. Section 2, Par. 2, Section 4 Pars. 1, 3 and 4,
    Sections 5, 6 Par. 1 and Section 7 of the
    First Decree to the Reich Citizens Law of No-
    vember 14, 1935 (REICHSGESETZBLATT I p. 1333).

Section 2.

The date on which Section 1 Par. 2 of the Reich
Citizens Law becomes effective will be decided by the
Reich Minister of the Interior.

Section 3.

The exclusion of Jews from public offices which
they occupy at the time this decree goes into effect
will be specially regulated.

Section 4

Section 4.

In the Province of Austria September 16, 1935,
will also be deemed the date of issuance of the Reich
Citizens Law, as far as the application of Section 5
Par.2 of the First Decree to the Reich Citizens Law is
concerned, and September 17, 1935, as the day on which the
Law for the Protection of German Blood and German Honor
became effective.

Article II
Law for the Protection of German
Blood.

Section 5.

The following apply in the Province of Austria:
the Law for the Protection of German Blood and German
Honor of September 15, 1935 (REICHSGESETZBLATT I page
1146) and the First Decree for the Execution of this
Law of November 14, 1935 (REICHSGESETZBLATT I page 1334).

Section 6.

Section 3 of the Law for the Protection of German
Blood goes into effect on August 1, 1938.

Section 7.

In the Province of Austria September 16, 1935, shall
also be deemed the date of issuance of the Law for the
Protection of German Blood, as far as the application of
Section 12, Par.3 of the First Executory Decree to the
Law for the Protection of Blood is concerned.

Section 8.

(1) No marriage must be contracted before it is
proved by means of a certificate of the mayor locally competent for the regular domicile of the fiancee that no impediment to a marriage exists according to the Law for

the

the Protection of German Blood and to the First Executory Decree to that Law.   If the fiancée has no regular domicile in the Province of Austria, the competency
of the mayor is governed by the provisions of Section 3
of the General Law governing Administrative Procedure
(Österreichisches BGBL. No. 274-1925).

(2)   If the mayor has any doubts as to the existence of an impediment to a marriage in the meaning of
Section 6 of the First Executory Decree to the Law for
the Protection of German Blood, he must demand of the
couple to be married that they present a certificate
regarding their fitness for marriage (Ehetauglichkeitszeugnis) of the official physician.

Section 9.

Regarding the application of Section 15, sentence 2
of the First Executory Decree to the Law for the Protection of German Blood, former possession of Austrian Federal citizenship is on a par with the former possession
of German nationality.

Article III
Regulations for Procedure

Section 10

The provisions of Austrian law governing competency
and the procedure of the courts in legal disputes concerning the nullification of a marriage apply to action for
nullity mutatis mutandis with the following provisos:

1.   The action must be brought against both husband
and wife.   If the State's Attorney or one of

the

125

the marital partners appeals, both marital partners must be considered the opponent, in the first case, and in the second, the State's Attorney and the other marital partner.

2. The regulation governing the compulsion to be represented by a lawyer does not apply to the State's Attorney.

.3. If the State's Attorney is defeated, the public treasury must be sentenced to refund the costs incurred by the couple, in accordance with Sections 40 et seq. of the Austrian Civil Procedure Code.

4. No marriage bond counsel will be appointed (Ehebandsverteidiger).

5. Action can only be brought while both marital partners are living. If one of the marital partner dies before the judgment becomes absolute, the case is to be regarded as settled, in principle.

Section 11

The tribunal of first instance is competent for contraventions of Section 5 Pars. 1 and 2 of the Law for the Protection of German Blood.

Article IV

Final Provisions

Section 12

In cases where provisions which are introduced in the Province of Austria through this decree cannot be applied direct, they must be applied mutatis mutandis.

Section 13.

Section 13.

This decree goes into effect on the day after
its promulgation.

Berlin, May 20, 1938.

The Reich Minister of the Interior

Frick

The Deputy of the Führer

R. Hess

The Reich Minister of Justice

Dr. Schlegelberger, Acting.

AC:EM

STAFF EVIDENCE ANALYSIS, Ministries Group   By: G. Schwab
                                             Date: 1 November 1946.

Document Number: NG-347

Title and or general nature: Correspondence between the Minis-
                                   try of the Interior and the Min-
                                   istries of Justice and Economics,
                                   concerning a contemplated Extension
                                   of the Law for the Protection of
                                   German Blood ("Blutschutzgesetz")
                                   designed to prevent German
                                   women from being employed in
                                   Jewish Clothing Concerns.

Form of Document: A) copy of letter
                                   B) copy of letter
                                   C) Original of letter.

Stamps and other endorsements: A) Stamp of Ministry of Interior
                                   B) None.
                                   C) Stamp of Ministry of Interior

Date: A) 25 May 1938
                                   B) 22 September 1938
                                   C) 6 December 1938

Source: Original; Reichsjustizministerium General-
                                   akten ueber Blutschutzgesetz
                                   Strafrechtlich Fragen, Band 1
                                   1120/1; Photostat on file in
                                   Doc. Room, OCC, Nuernberg.
                                   Now at: Reichspatentamt, Berlin.
                                        (OCC BBT 529 A,B and C.

PERSONS OR ORGANIZATIONS IMPLICATED:

                                   SCHLEGELBERGER
                                   SCHAEFER, Dr, Ministerialdirigent
                                   KLEMM, Ministerialrat
                                   ROTHENBERGER (?)
                                   RICHTER, Dr. Ministerialrat
                                   LOESENER, Ministry of Interior
                                   HERING, Ministry of Interior
                                   METTGENBERG, Dr,
                                   PFUNDTNER, State Secretary in
                                             Ministry of Interior
                                   Ministry of Economics

TO BE FILED UNDER THESE REFERENCE HEADINGS:

                                   NG - Ministry of Justice
                                   NG - Ministry of the Interior
                                   NG - Racial Persecution

SUMMARY:

A)   In this letter from PFUNDTNER to the Deputy of the Fuehrer,
      the writer refers to the necessity of supplementing the Law
      for the Protection of German Blood (Blutschutzgesetz), which
      provides that German females under 45 years of age are not
      allowed to work in Jewish households. The writer wants his law

supplemented in such a way that German woman under 45 will
not be allowed to work in a great number of Jewish industries
and enterprises such as hotels and tailorshops. He also speaks
of other measures planned against the Jews and also proposes
the introduction of the Nuernberg Racial Laws in Austria
as soon as possible.

B)   This letter from the Ministry of the Interior, signed
by LOESENER, to the Minister of Economics points out the
necessity of supplementing the law for the Protection of
German Blood (Blutschutzgesetz) so that in the future German
women under 45 will not be able to work in the Jewish
clothing industry. The writer also states that the problem would
solve itself, if plans for the general closing of Jewish industries were carried out.

C)   This letter from the Ministry of the Interior to the
Ministry of Justice refers to the letter of 22 September 1938
(A); the writer states that since the complete elimination
of the Jews from the industry will be completed shortly,
there is no need for further supplementary laws to the
"Blutschutzgesetz".

129

Copy.

The Reich and Prussian

Minister of the Interior

I c 124 II/38
5017

In reply please refer to
number and subject

Rubber stamp:

Berlin, 25 May 1938
NW 40, Koenigsplatz 6
illegible print

Reich Ministry of
Justice
26 May 1938

initials

To

the Deputy Fuehrer

M u n i c h
The Brown House

Subject: Supplement to Article 3 of the Law for the Protection
of German Blood and Honor. In reply to the letter of
14 April 1939 – III/04 – Ku –
2430/0

I too deem a supplement to Article 3 of the Law for the Protect-

ion of German Blood and Honor necessary in the sense indicated in

your letter of 26 February 1938 – III/04 Mue. 2430/0.II am inclosing

a draft of a decree to that effect. By virtue of that decree, as

it stands now, the following would be prohibited:

1)   The employment altogether of women of German blood and below

     45 years by Jewish tailors, restaurants, boarding houses, private

     hotels, hotels, sanatoriums and health resorts;

2)   the employment by all other Jews and Jewish enterprises of female

     private secretaries, receptionists of doctors, buyers, travelling

     agents and companions, as well as models, of German blood and

     below 45 years. It remains to be discussed if this ban should

     be extended to female office employees, steno-typists, and similar

     commercial employees, particularly to those specially trusted posi-

tions.Finally it would have to be decided upon when this employment

ban is to become effective and if a relaxation of the ban is deemed

advisable with regard to employees over 35 years – similar to the

provisions of Article 12 of the first implementation ordinance of

– 1 –

(page 1 of original, cont'd)

the Law for the Protection of German Blood and Honor,.

As, according to information received from your deputy,

Reichsamtsleiter Dr. BLOME, the Fuehrer and Reich Chancellor

To the   does not desire the Nuernberg Racial Laws to be amended at
Herr Reich
Minister   the present time, I have refrained so far,
of Justice;

handwritten:
1120/1 - IIa -   (page 2 of original)
   660/38

BBT - 529   NG -347.

from submitting this ordinance. Quite apart from that, I think it much

more appropriate to introduce first of all the Nuernberg Racial Laws as

they stand in Austria as soon as possible, in order to remedy the gross-

est abuses, in the field of race, in Austria. This already will mean

a great increase of work for my Ministry in the near future, because

of the expected applications asking for exceptions to be made. Simul-

taneously the legislative measures concerning Jewish economy, of which

you know, must also be carried out as soon as possible. That requires

necessarily the postponement of all other measures planned in connection

with the Jews. However I hope that soon these pressing tasks will have

advanced far enough so that the required supplement, suggested by you,

to Article 3 of the Law for the Protection of German Blood and Honor can

be dealt with.

File   -In reply to your letter of 3 January 1938 - 1120/1 - II a 2 1 -

142 A   38, I am respectfully forwarding this copy for information.

signed: PFUNDTNER

as deputy

- 2 -

(page 2 of original, cont'd)

handwritten:

1) To State secretary FREISLER
   with the request to report in person

2) Re-submit in 4 weeks.

	Rubber stamp:	national emblem with inscription.	Certified: Signature Clerk of the Registry.

132

(page 3 of original)

Copy to No $\underline{\dfrac{I e 124 VI/38}{5017}}$

The Reich Minister of the Interior   Berlin, 22 September 1938.
    No $\underline{\dfrac{I e 124 IV/38}{5017}}$

To the

    Reich Minister of Economy

    B e r l i n .

    Subject: Supplement to the Law for the Protection of German
               Blood and Honor. In reply to your letter of
               6 September 1938 - III Jd. 5152/38.

        As far back as the end of last year, I started on a draft
of a supplement to Article 3 of the Law for the Protection of
German Blood and Honor. At the same time, I had inquiries made to
ascertain if and to what extent violations of that law, with regard
to employment of women of German blood in the clothing industry,
have led to police action and criminal proceedings. These inquiries have shown that an extension in that direction of the employment ban is required. But the matter was deferred again this
May, because, according to information received from the Deputy
Fuehrer, the Fuehrer and Reich Chancellor did not desire at that
time the Nuernberg Racial Laws to be amended. It is intended to
submit the matter again in due time to the Fuehrer for a decision.
I shall take the liberty of communicating with you then again.

        May I point out that the whole question will be settled to
a large degree with the realization of the plans aiming at the
general closing down of Jewish enterprises. Therefore I think it
useful to wait, first of all, for a decision on these plans.

                                    By order
handwritten:
file with 1120/1-IIa^2_   signed: Dr. LOESENER
    17 Nov 38.
                            - 4 -

133

(page 4 of original)

The Reich Minister of the Interior

No I e 124 VI/38
        5017

In reply please refer
to number and subject

Berlin, 6 December 1938.
NW 40, Koenigsplatz 6
illegible print
Telephone numbers

Rubberstamp: a 12 December 1938

Rubberstamp:
Reich Ministry of Justice
3 December 1938
initials

To the Herr
Reich Minister of Justice

B e r l i n .

Subject: Supplement to Article 3 of the Law for the Protection
           of German Blood and Honor. In reply to your letter
           of 22 November 1938 - 1120/1 - IIa^2 1623.38.

134

For your information as to the stand of matters, please

find inclosed a copy of the letter of 22 September 1938

± I e 124 IV/38 - 5017, addressed to the Reich Minister of

Economy. As within the near future the general elimination of

the Jews from the German economy can be expected, I do not

intend

handwritten: 1120/1 - I Ia^2 - 17 Nov 38   Inclosure: 1

(page 2 of original)

to follow up the then proposed supplement to the Law for the

Protection of German Blood and Honor.

By order

signed: HERING

Rubberstamp: emblem, inscribed:
              Reich Ministry of
              the Interior.

Certified:
signed: STREITER
Secretary of the
ministerial
chancellory.

1) State secretary FREISLER for information.

2) To be filed

CERTIFICATE OF TRANSLATION

29 January 1948

I, Kurt SCHREUER, Civ.No.35 299, hereby certify that I am a duly appointed translator for the German and English languages and that the above is a true and correct translation of document No NG-347.

. . . .
Kurt SCHREUER
Civ.No.35 299

135

TELEGRAM RECEIVED

GRAY

Berlin

FROM Dated June 16, 1938

Rec'd 9 a.m.

Secretary of State,

Washington.

307, June 16, 11 a.m.

Evidence is received that since the beginning of
the week a fairly large scale series of arrests of Jews
has been carried out in Berlin and, according to some
reports, in other cities as well. It appears that those
arrested are Jews whose names appear on the police records
in connection with earlier investigations and offenses
including those of the most minor kind presumably settled
some time ago. No information is given concerning the
number of arrests, the charges to be brought, or the dis-
position to be made of the prisoners, although it is understood that the latter are being submitted to physical
examinations to determine possibly if they might be sent
to concentration camps or be employed to perform forced
manual labor.

Jewish leaders are of the opinion that this new
wave of persecution which is being directed by the police
instead of as formerly by the uniformed party groups can
only be intended to encourage emigration. In this latter

connection

-2- #307, June 16, 11 a.m. from Berlin

connection attention is called to a German press report
of last week that at the present rate of emigration thirty
years would be required before the last Jew had left
Germany.

137

WILSON

WWC:DDM

DEPARTMENT OF STATE

DIVISION OF EUROPEAN AFFAIRS

July 8, 1938.

Summary of Despatch No. 196, from Embassy at Berlin, dated June 22, 1938.

Subject: Demonstrations Against Jewish Shops.

Following the large-scale arrest of Jews in Germany during the early part of June, organized demonstrations in Berlin against Jewish shopkeepers occurred on the week end of June 18. The day before Jewish shop owners had been ordered to display their names in white letters, and this made the task of those who went about painting "Jude" on these shops all easier. It is the opinion of informed sections of the public that this action was carried out by representatives of the Labor Front rather than the S.A. or the S.S. as has formerly been the case. There are reports of several incidents of the looting of shops and the beating up of their owners, and empty show case windows lend credence to these reports. This is the first attempt since 1933 to revive organized marking and picketing of Jewish shops.

The German News Bureau claimed that the raids were directed exclusively against criminal

- 2 -

criminal elements and were not in the least motivated by political considerations. It was admitted, however, that a number of Jews had been taken into custody for their own safety to protect them against growing popular indignation caused by a new influx of Jews to the capital, where the latter had evidently hoped to escape observation. The Völkischer Beobachter mentioned that over three thousand Jews had come to Berlin during the last month.

In addition to the marking of shops, the Minister of Economics made public on June 21 an order forbidding Jewish traders further access to German stock exchanges and commodity markets. However, in the interests of general economy, Jewish traders will be permitted to operate for the time being through properly empowered "Aryan" associates.

The present anti-Jewish campaign outstrips in thoroughness anything of the kind since 1933. The current drive is evidently being fanned by the suspicion that many Austrian Jews may have come to Berlin to seek refuge and by the feeling that emigration has been too slow. It is expected that the present campaign will also bring forth further legislative measures. In this connection certain foreign correspondents in Berlin state that they have been informed that the window-painting measures have been called off by the Party.

One

One measure which is proving effective in anticipation of more general and legal steps is the practice which is known to have been followed whereby a Party member will approach the Jewish owner of a prosperous business and will "advise" him to sell out at a price named arbitrarily by the prospective "Aryan" purchaser (often the Party member himself).

EMBASSY OF THE
UNITED STATES OF AMERICA

No. 196   Berlin, June 22, 1938.

Subject: Demonstrations Against Jewish Shops.

The Honorable

The Secretary of State,

Washington.

Sir:

With reference to the Embassy's telegram
No. 307 of June 16, 11 a.m., reporting large
scale arrests of Jews, I have the honor to inform the Department that this action was followed on the week-end of June 18 by organized
demonstrations in Berlin against Jewish shopkeepers.

Starting late Saturday afternoon, civilian groups, consisting usually of two or three men,
were to be observed painting on the windows of
Jewish shops the word "JUDE" in large red letters,
the Star of David and caricatures of Jews. On the
Kurfürstendamm and the Tauentzienstrasse, the fash-
ionable shopping districts in the West, the task

of

of the painters was made easy by the fact that Jewish shop-owners had been ordered the day before to
display their names in white letters. (This step,
which was evidently decreed in anticipation of a
forthcoming ruling which will require Jews to display a uniform distinctive sign, disclosed that a
surprisingly large number of shops in this district
are still Jewish.) The painters in each case were
followed by large groups of spectators who seemed to
enjoy the proceedings thoroughly. The opinion in informed sections of the public was that the task was
being undertaken by representatives of the Labor
Front rather than as formerly has been the case by
the S.A. or the S.S. It is understood that in
the district around the Alexanderplatz boys of the
Hitler Youth participated in the painting, making
up for their lack of skill by a certain imagination
and thoroughness of mutilation. Reports are received
that several incidents took place in this region
leading to the looting of shops and the beating up
of their owners; a dozen or so broken and empty
show cases and windows have been seen which lend
credence to these reports.

A tour of the city on Sunday betrayed a sorry
spectacle particularly in those districts inhabited
by Jews where practically the only persons to be
seen were policemen patrolling the vacant and be-
smirched streets. On Monday most of the owners of
the painted shops in the West End had cleaned off

the

the signs except in the case of the large stores
of Rosenhain and Grünfeld which have long been the
envy of their competitors, where a picket by small
boys and evil-looking vagrants is still being maintained.   On the whole, five years of Jew-baiting
in Berlin seems to have exhausted the originality
of the methods of public demonstration although
the latest measures are significant as being the
first attempt since 1933 to revive organized marking and picketing of Jewish shops.

Incidentally it is learned that at least four
foreign correspondents, including three Americans
and an Englishman, were arrested for taking pictures of the painted Jewish shops.   After making
known their identity and insisting that they were
unaware of any law making it illegal to take pictures of this nature, they were released although
it is understood that the automobile and camera of
the English journalist were provisionally held by
the police.

The DEUTSCHES NACHRICHTEN BÜRO on Saturday,
June 18, published a communique with respect to
the arrests of last week.   It is stated that in
continuation of the series of raids at the end of
May which had gathered in 317 suspect Jews, a number of new arrests had been carried out on June 16
resulting in the apprehension of 143 additional
Jews.   The DEUTSCHES NACHRICHTEN BÜRO claimed

that

141

that the raids were directed exclusively against
criminal elements and were not in the least motivated by political considerations. It was admitted,
however, that a number of Jews had been taken into
custody for their own safety to protect them against
growing popular indignation caused by a new influx
of Jews to the capital where the latter had evidently
hoped to escape observation. With respect to those
arrested it appears that while some of the aged and
infirm have been released, the number of Jews still
held remains about the same, reaching possibly a total of several hundred; it is understood that those
who do not reside permanently in Berlin will be
shipped back to the communities from whence they came
and that others may be sent to a new work camp near
Weimar.

On June 21, after the peak of the demonstrations had momentarily passed, the VÖLKISCHER BEOB-
ACHTER sought to make short work at one and the same
time of the Jews and the foreign press which was por-
trayed as rushing to their aid. Mentioning that
over 3,000 Jews had come to Berlin during the last
month, the VÖLKISCHER BEOBACHTER editorially declared that the population had been forced to adopt
measures of self-help particularly as the Jews had
taken to insulting women on the street. In the
same issue of the paper, Karl Megerle, known chief-
ly for his writings on foreign politics in the

BOERSENZEITUNG

142

BOERSENZEITUNG, compares the moderation of the present measures against the Jews with the outrages perpetrated against the German people by the allied troops of occupation in the Rhineland and the Ruhr which had escaped all mention in the foreign press of that time.

To the already long list of anti-Jewish repressive measures is to be added the order of the Minister of Economics made public June 21 forbidding Jewish traders further access to German stock exchanges and commodity markets; in the interests of general economy the Jewish traders will be permitted, however, to operate for the time being through properly empowered "Aryan" associates. On the same date it was announced that the postoffices would cease to deliver advertising matter posted by Jewish firms at the usual cheap mail rates, unless this material was addressed to Jewish clients or firms.

In conclusion it may be said that the present anti-Jewish campaign outstrips in thoroughness anything of the kind since early 1933, extending beyond a mere summer exuberance of the Party such as made itself manifest in 1935. Doubtless set off in the first instance by the taking over of the Austrian Jewish population, the current drive is evidently being fanned by the suspicion that many Austrian Jews may have come to Berlin to seek refuge, and by the feeling that emigration has been altogether too slow. Just as the outbursts of 1935 led to the

143

Nuremberg

Nuremberg legislation of September of that year, it is expected that the present campaign will also bring forth further legislative measures, and in this connection reference is made to the very clear prediction made by Dr. Goebbels in his speech delivered at the "Summer Solstice Ceremonies" in the Olympic Stadium on June 21.

• As reported by the 12 UHR BLATT, Dr. Goebbels inquired: "Is it not altogether outrageous, and does it not bring a blush of rage to one's face, that in the last month no less than three thousand Jews have emigrated to Berlin? What do they want here?" Dr. Goebbels then said that the task of dealing with the "international Jewry" in Berlin would be carried out according to Party and State laws and not on the street. Legal measures would be provided which in the foreseeable future would break Jewish influence in German economy. Dr. Goebbels "begged" the Jewish population not to act so provocatively in public and "demanded" the general public to maintain its discipline. (In this connection local foreign correspondents state that they have been informed that the "active measures," such as the window-painting of last week, have been called off by the Party.)

It is regarded as possible that the predicted legislation may come after the registration of Jewish property has been completed on June 30 in accordance with the recent decree and may be announced

at

at the forthcoming Party Congress in September,
if not before.   One measure which is proving effective in anticipation of more general and legal
steps is the practice which is known to have been
followed in several instances whereby a Party member will approach the Jewish owner of a prosperous
business and will "advise" him to sell out at a
price named arbitrarily by the prospective "Aryan"
purchaser (often the Party member himself).

Respectfully yours,

Hugh R. Wilson

800
JDB:EM

145

No. 292, dated Oct. 26, 1938
from the American Embassy,
Berlin, Germany.

Translation
from
REICHSGESETZBLATT I, No. 165
October 14, 1938

Fifth Decree governing Reich Citizenship Law
dated September 27, 1938.

On the basis of Section 3 of the Reich Citizenship
Law of September 15, 1935 (REICHSGESETZBLATT, Part I,
page 1146), the following is decreed:

Article I.

Elimination of Jews from Corps of Lawyers

Section 1.

The profession of lawyer is closed to Jews. In so
far as Jews are still lawyers they are eliminated from
the Corps of Lawyers in accordance with the following
regulations:

a) In the old Reich territory:

> The licenses of Jewish lawyers are to be
> revoked as of November 30, 1938;

b) In the Province of Austria:

> 1. Jewish lawyers are to be stricken from
> the list of lawyers at the latest by Decem-
> ber 31, 1938, by order of the Reich Minister
> of Justice.
>
> 2. In the case of Jews who are registered in
> the list of the Lawyers' Chamber in Vienna,
> cancellation may be waived for the time
> being if their families have been in the
> Province of Austria for at least fifty years,
> and if they were front line fighters.   The
> date of cancellation in this case is deter-
> mined by the Reich Minister of Justice.
>
> 3. Until a decision is reached concerning
> whether cancellation from the list of lawyers
> is to take place, the Reich Minister of Jus-
> tice may provisionally forbid a lawyer the
> exercise of his profession.

Section

Section 2.

(1) Contracts for services which, a Jew eliminated from the Corps of Lawyers in accordance with this decree had concluded when he was entitled to do so, may be terminated by both parties upon three months' notice for the end of any calendar month, even if a longer period for giving notice was stipulated legally or contractually or if the service relationship was entered into for a definite period.

(2) Notice according to Par. (1) may be given

a) In the old territory of the Reich only for February 28, 1939,

b) In the Province of Austria only for the earliest date for which it may be given after the date on which the former lawyer or his employee receives notification of cancellation from the list of lawyers.

(3) Legal or contractual regulations concerning a shorter period for giving notice than that provided in Par. (1) remain unaffected.

Section 3.

(1) Whoever is eliminated from the Corps of Lawyers on the basis of this decree may, within the legally prescribed time limit, give notice to terminate the lease of rooms which he has rented for himself or his family, notwithstanding contrary agreements concerning the term of the lease or the time limit for giving notice. The same applies to employees of a lawyer who become unemployed owing to the fact that the lawyer is eliminated from the Corps of Lawyers as a result of this decree.

147

(2)

(2) Notice may be given by a lawyer in accordance with Par. (1):

    a) in the old territory of the Reich, only on the first date for which it is permissible after November 30, 1938,

    b) in the Province of Austria, only on the first date for which it is permissible after the date on which the lawyer was informed of his cancellation from the list of lawyers.

.(3) The employee may give notice in accordance with Par. (1) only for the first date for which notice is permissible after termination of his employment.

(4) Furthermore, the following applies mutatis mutandis to giving notice:

    a) In the old territory of the Reich, the provisions of Section 6 of the law of April 7, 1933, concerning admission to the Corps of Lawyers (REICHSGESETZBLATT, Part I, page 188);

    b) In the Province of Austria, the provisions of Section 13 of the decree of May 31, 1938, for the reorganization of the Austrian Civil Service (REICHSGESETZBLATT, Part I, page 607).

Section 4.

a) Jews eliminated from the Corps of Lawyers on the basis of this decree are forbidden to attend to legal matters for others in accordance with Article I, Section 8 of the law of December 13, 1935, for the prevention of misusage in the field of legal davice.

b) In the Province of Austria, until the law for the prevention of misusages in the field of legal advice becomes effective, the following applies:

    1. Whoever has been stricken off the list of Lawyers on the basis of this decree may no longer attend to legal matters for others on a business basis; in particular. he is not permitted to represent clients in court or out of court, to give them legal advice or to collect claims for them.

2.

2. Courts or other authorities may not entrust a former lawyer with the administration or realization of the property of others. If an order of this sort has already been given him, the authority which appointed him must cancel the order and must transfer the order to another lawyer or other suitable person, in so far as this appears necessary for the prevention of legal disadvantages for those involved, or for any other reason.

3. The regulations in Nos. 1 and 2 do not apply to the own affairs of the former lawyer and those of his wife and minor children in so far as the employment of a lawyer is not compulsory.

4. Whoever deliberately contravenes the regulations of No. 1 will be punished with a fine.

5. For the period of a provisional prohibition of the exercise of the profession, the regulations in Nos. 1 to 4 apply mutatis mutandis.

Section 5.

Jews eliminated from the Corps of Lawyers on the basis of this decree, in so far as they were front line fighters and in case of need and worthiness, may be granted maintenance contributions, recallable at any time, from the revenues of the Jewish Legal Advisers (Section 14).   Under like premises other Jews eliminated from the Corps of Lawyers on the basis of this decree may also be granted maintenance contributions of this kind within the limits of the sums paid in, if they have been registered in the list of lawyers since August 1, 1914.

Section 6.

(1) A front line fighter in the meaning of this decree is one who in the World War (in the period from August 1, 1914 to December 31, 1918) participated in a battle, fight, entrenched conflict or siege with the

fighting

149

fighting troops on the side of the German Reich or its Allies. It is not sufficient if some one was present in the war zone on duty during the war without having faced the enemy.

(2) Participation in the fighting which took place after the World War in the Baltic district or against the enemies of the National uprising or for the defence of German soil is equal to participation in the fighting of the World War.

Article II.

Cancellation of Jews from the Lists of Those Intending to Become Lawyers and of Legal Defenders in the Province of Austria.

Section 7.

150

(1) Jews will no longer be entered in the lists of those intending to become lawyers and of defenders in criminal matters. In so far as Jews are still entered in these lists they will be canceled at the latest by December 31, 1938 by order of the Reich Minister of Justice.'

(2) The provisions of Article I, Section 1, letter b, No. 3, and Sections 2 to 4 of this decree apply mutatis mutandis.

Article III

Legal Advice and Representation of Jews

Section 8.

The Administration of Justice permits Jewish legal advisers (jüdische Konsulenten) to represent and to give legal advice to Jews.

Section

Section 9.

(1) Jewish advisers will only be permitted in so far as there is need thereof.

(2) The permission is subject to recall. For the purpose of substitution of a Jewish adviser who has been approved, a permit may be issued temporarily.

(3) The Jewish advisers and their substitutes are to be taken, as far as possible, from among those Jews who are eliminated from the Corps of Lawyers in accordance with Section 1 of this decree; front line fighters are to be given preference as far as possible.

Section 10.

Jewish advisers may attend professionally only to the legal affairs of Jews as well as of Jewish firms, Jewish associations, funds, institutions and other Jewish undertakings. In particular, they may undertake to give legal advice to the above-mentioned parties only and to represent them in or out of court, as well as to collect claims for them.

Section 11.

(1) Jewish advisers will be allotted a definite locality for their professional establishment. The maintenance of branch establishments, outside office hours, or similar permanent arrangements in another locality takes place in accordance with detailed regulations of the Administration of Justice.

(2) In so far as Jewish advisers are permitted to attend to legal matters, they may be active in a dis-

trict

151

trict to be determined by the Administration of Justice
before all courts and administrative authorities as well
as before all courts and authorities superior to these
and may act as authorized attorneys also vis-à-vis the
opponents of their clients.   This also applies in so
far as lawyers may only participate in proceedings if
they are admitted to the court before which the proceedings take place; in so far as further restrictive regulations exist, they apply mutatis mutandis.

(3) Otherwise the professional activity of Jewish
advisers is not subject to any local restrictions.

Section 12.

Jewish advisers may be appointed under the provisions for paupers, as emergency representatives (in
accordance with Section 38 of the Reich Lawyers' Law)
or as official defenders.   In so far as legal regulations having to do with procedure, in particular Sections 135, 198, 212 a, of the Reich Civil Procedure
Code, envisage simplifications and other details for
lawyers, they apply to Jewish advisers mutatis mutandis.

Section 13.

The Jewish advisers are subject to the supervision
of the Administration of Justice.

Section 14.

(1) From their clients the Jewish advisers collect
in their own name, but for the account of a clearing
office to be determined by the Reich Minister of Justice,
fees and expenditures in accordance with the Reich and

State

State legal regulations in force for lawyers. Opponents
of the Jewish client who are liable for costs are to
pay these sums in the same manner as the costs of a
lawyer.

(2) There remains for the Jewish advisers as compensation for their professional activity and as remuner-
ation for chancery costs - in addition to refunds for
necessary cash outlays for travel, etc. - a share of the
fees resulting from their professional activities.

(3) From the sums flowing into the clearing office
the maintenance contributions payable under Section 5
of this decree will be paid.

(4) Detailed regulations may be issued through
general administrative orders.

153

Article IV

Final and Transitional Regulations

Section 15.

(1) If in a civil legal matter the lawyer of one
of the parties becomes incapable through a measure
adopted on the basis of this decree of continuing the
representation of that party, proceedings in which
representation by a lawyer is not compulsory will also
be interrupted.

(2) An interruption of the proceedings, however,
does not take place if the lawyer is admitted as a Jewish adviser simultaneously with his elimination from the
Corps of Lawyers and in that capacity is allowed to
continue representing his client.

Section

Section 16.

To a party who in a civil legal matter or in a
criminal matter misses a proceeding set for a definite
date, or fails to undertake a measure in litigation
for which a definite date was set, is to be granted
the reestablishment of the previous status, on application, if he was prevented through measures adopted on
the basis of this decree from appearing on time for the
proceedings or from undertaking the step in litigation
on time.

Section 17.

(1) If an exchange of representatives occurs in
attending to a legal matter, owing to the elimination
of a Jew from the Corps of Lawyers on the basis of this
decree, the opponent of the client of the Jewish lawyer who is liable for costs is not obliged to refund the
additional costs arising from the exchange of representatives.

(2) If a Jewish adviser takes over a legal matter
hitherto attended to by a Jewish lawyer, he must credit
his client with the fees owed to the Jewish lawyer. The
Jewish adviser and the former Jewish lawyer must bring
about by an amicable agreement an adjustment concerning
the fees due the former lawyer if this is equitable in
view of the extent of work done by both in the legal
matter.   If an agreement is not reached, a decision
may arrived at with regard to such an adjustment through
administrative channels on application of either party
involved.

Section

154

Section 18.

To proceedings which are under way against a Jew
before a lawyers' court of honor at the time at which
he is eliminated from the Corps of Lawyers under this
decree, the regulations of Section 2 of the decree supplementing the regulations concerning procedure before
a court of honor against lawyers of August 31, 1937
(REICHSGESETZBLATT, Part I, page 919) apply mutatis
mutandis.

Section 19.

The Reich Minister of Justice is authorized to issue
the necessary legal and administrative regulations for
the execution and supplementing of this decree.   In so
far as the Reich Minister of Finance is involved they
will be issued in agreement with him.

Berlin, September 27, 1938.

155

> The Führer and Reich Chancelor
> Adolf Hitler
>
> The Reich Minister of Justice
> Dr. Gürtner
>
> The Reich Minister of the Interior
> Frick
>
> The Deputy of the Führer
> R. Hess
>
> The Reich Minister of Finance
>
> Reinhardt, Acting

HCF:AC:AC

EMBASSY OF THE
UNITED STATES OF AMERICA

No. 433   Berlin, November 17, 1938.

Subject: Transmitting Translations
of Three Decrees issued by
Field Marshal Göring rela-
tive to the Economic Situation of Jews in Germany.

Doc. 16

156

The Honorable

The Secretary of State,

Washington.

A-M/C

RECORDING DESK
FILE - C.

I have the honor to enclose herewith transla-

tions, prepared by the Embassy, of the following

three decrees issued by Field Marshal Göring, act-

ing in his capacity as Commissioner of the Four

Year Plan, which were published in REICHSGESETZBLATT

Part I, No. 189, of November 14, 1938 (only received

by the Embassy this morning).

1/   (a)   Decree covering payment of a fine by
                Jews of German nationality, dated No-
                vember 12, 1938.

2/   (b)   Decree to eliminate the Jews from
                German economic life, dated November
                12, 1938.

3/   (c)   Decree for the restoration of the ap-
                pearance of the streets in the case
                of Jewish business enterprises, dated
                November 12, 1938.

                                    (4) There

4/   There is also enclosed a translation of the communique announcing these decrees, which was issued by the German News Agency and was published in the German press on November 13, 1928.

Due to the pressure of other work of more immediate urgency, it has thus far been impossible to complete, as a supplement to the Embassy's numerous telegrams on the subject, a despatch relating to the various phases of the current intensification of Germany's anti-Jewish policy. Such a despatch, however, is now in the process of preparation and will be forwarded to the Department as soon as possible.

In accordance with the Department's instruction, two copies of this despatch and its enclosures are being forwarded to the Intergovernmental Committee for Political Refugees, London.

157

Respectfully yours,

Prentiss Gilbert
Chargé d'Affaires ad interim.

Enclosures:
   1-2-3. Translations of Decrees,
      as above.
   4. Translation of communique.

800

Two copies to Intergovernmental
Committee for Political Refugees,
c/o American Embassy, London.

HPL:EM

Decree Covering Payment of a Fine
by Jews of German Nationality, of
November 12, 1938.

The inimical attitude of the Jews towards
the German people and Reich, which does not even
• hesitate to commit dastardly murders, calls for
a definite defensive and severe expiation.

I therefore decree on the basis of the Decree
of October 18, 1936, for the Execution of the Four
Year Plan (RGB I page 887) as follows:

158

Section 1.

Payment of a contribution of one billion marks
to the German Reich is imposed upon the Jews of
German nationality in their entirety.

Section 2.

The executory regulations will be issued by
the Reich Minister of Finance in conjunction with
the Reich Ministers concerned.

AC:EM

Decree to Eliminate the Jews from
German Economic Life, dated November
12, 1938.

Section 1.

As from January 1, 1939, Jews (Section 5
of the First Decree to the Reich Citizen Law of November 14, 1935, RGB I page 1333) will be prohibited
from operating retail stores, distributing and mail
order houses or delivery offices, and from carrying
on a trade independently.

Furthermore, as from the same date they are prohibited from offering goods or industrial services at
markets of any kind, fairs or exhibitions, from advertising them or from accepting orders for them.

Jewish business houses (Third Decree to the Reich
Citizen Law of June 14, 1938 - RGB I page 627), carried
on in contravention of this prohibition must be closed
by the police.

Section 2.

After January 1, 1939, no Jew can be a plant manager in the meaning of the Law of January 20,1934, Regulating National Labor (RGB I p.45).

If a Jew is engaged in an economic undertaking as
a leading employee, he can be given 6 weeks' notice.
Upon the expiration of this time limit all claims accru-
ing to the employee from the denounced contract, particularly also claims to maintenance allowances and compensation, expire.

Section 3.

159

Section 3.

A Jew may not be a member of a cooperative
society. Jewish members of cooperative societies
retire on December 31, 1938. No special notice
is required.

Section 4.

The competent Reich ministers are authorized
to issue the executory regulations necessary for the
performance of this decree. They may allow exceptions, where they are necessary as a result of trans-
fering a Jewish concern to non-Jewish ownership,for
liquidating Jewish concerns or, in special cases, to
insure the supply.

Berlin, November 12, 1938.

160

The Commissioner for the Four Year Plan
Göring
Field Marshal General

AC:EM

Decree for the Restoration of the
Appearance of the Streets in the
Case of Jewish Business Enterprises,
dated November 12,1938.

Section 1.

All damages which were caused to Jewish business
houses and dwellings by the revolt of the people against
the agitation of international Jewry, against National
Socialist Germany on November 8, 9 and 10, must be remedied immediately by the Jewish owners or Jewish business
people.

Section 2.

The costs of repairs must be borne by the owners of the Jewish business houses and dwellings.

Insurance claims of Jews of German nationality
will be confiscated in favor of the Reich.

Section 3.

The Reich Minister of Economics is authorized to
issue executory regulations in agreement with the
Reich Ministers concerned.

161

AC:EM

Translation of German News Agency Communiqué
as published in the BERLINER BÖRSEN ZEITUNG
November 13, 1938.

One Billion Marks Penalty for Paris Murder.
Three Decrees of Göring concerning Compensation
Payments by Jews of German Nationality.

Under the chairmanship of Field Marshal Göring,
the Commissioner for the Four Year Plan, a meeting was
held today in the Reich Air Ministry at which the ministers concerned and their more immediate collabora-
tors discussed the urgent necessity of solving the
Jewish question. Reich Ministers Dr. Frick, Dr.Goeb-
bels, Dr. Gürtner, Count Schwerin-Krosigk, and Funk
participated in this discussion.

The result of the discussion was absolute unanim-
ity in judging and dealing with the question up for
discussion. A number of far-reaching measures to
solve the Jewish question were discussed and some of
them have already been decided upon. Field Marchal
Göring, the Commissioner for the Four Year Plan, issued a decree according to which Jews will be prohibited from operating retail stores, distributing and
mail order houses or delivery offices, and from carrying on a trade independently after January 1,1939.
Likewise under this decree a Jew will not be allowed
to function as a plant manager in the meaning of the
Law of January 1, 1934, Regulating National Labor,
after January 1, 1939. If a Jew holds a leading post
in an economic undertaking without being a plant manager, the relationship can be terminated by the plant
manager upon 6 weeks' notice.

The

162

The Commissioner for the Four Year Plan furthermore issued a decree according to which all damages to Jewish concerns and dwellings caused by the revolt of the nation against the agitation of international Jewry against National Socialist Germany on November 8, 9, and 10, 1938, must be remedied immediately by the Jewish owners or the Jewish business people. The costs of repairs must be carried by the owners of the Jewish business places or dwellings concerned.

Insurance claims of Jews of German nationality will be confiscated in favor of the Reich.

Further vitally important measures for eliminating Jews from the German economic life and to put an end to provocative conditions will be taken in the near future in the form of decrees and laws. Above all else, the decision was taken to impose upon the German Jews in their entirety a penalty for the ruthless murder in Paris in the shape of a fine amounting to one billion reichmarks. This whole amount will accrue to the Reich. The Commissioner for the Four Year Plan has already issued a decree to that effect.

163

AC:EM

OFFICE OF CHIEF OF COUNSEL
FOR WAR CRIMES
APO 124-A • U.S. ARMY

STAFF EVIDENCE ANALYSIS, Ministries Division.　　By: Dr. CORSING
　　　　　　　　　　　　　　　　　　　　　　　　　Date: Dec., 6, 1946.

Document Number:　　　　　　　　　NG-616

Title and/or general nature:　　　Measures concerning the "Aryani-
　　　　　　　　　　　　　　　　　　sation of Jewish Property in Nuern-
　　　　　　　　　　　　　　　　　　berg.

Form of Document:　　　　　　　　　Type-written reports, signed by
　　　　　　　　　　　　　　　　　　JOEL, Chief-Prosecuting-Attorney
　　　　　　　　　　　　　　　　　　(Special-Acts of the Ministry of
　　　　　　　　　　　　　　　　　　Justice)
　　　　　　　　　　　　　　　　　　　　A) February 15, 1939
　　　　　　　　　　　　　　　　　　　　B) February 16, 1939
　　　　　　　　　　　　　　　　　　　　D) report of LEISS (Amtsge-
　　　　　　　　　　　　　　　　　　　　　richtsrat) Nov. 28, 1938.

Stamps and other endorsements:　　--

Date:　　　　　　　　　　　　　　　A) February 15, 1939
　　　　　　　　　　　　　　　　　　B) February 16, 1939.

Source:　　　　　　　　　　　　　　Reichsjustizministerium,
　　　　　　　　　　　　　　　　　　149/XIII, Verhaeltnis der NSDAP
　　　　　　　　　　　　　　　　　　zur Rechtspflege.

　　　　　　　　　　　　　　　　　　now at: Reichspatentamt, Berlin.

　　　　　　　　　　　　　　　　　　OCC BBT 710.

PERSONS OR ORGANIZATIONS IMPLICATED:

　　　　　　　　　　　　　　　　　　Gaufachgruppenwalter NAGEL
　　　　　　　　　　　　　　　　　　President of the District-Court of
　　　　　　　　　　　　　　　　　　　Nuernberg, HOESCH
　　　　　　　　　　　　　　　　　　Secretary of State Dr. SCHLEGELBERGER
　　　　　　　　　　　　　　　　　　Amtsgerichtsdirektor Dr. GEREINER
　　　　　　　　　　　　　　　　　　　of Nuernberg
　　　　　　　　　　　　　　　　　　SA-Oberfuehrer KOENIG
　　　　　　　　　　　　　　　　　　Chief-Prosecuting-Attorney DENZLER

TO BE FILED UNDER THESE REFERENCE HEADINGS:

　　　　　　　　　　　　　　　　　　NG-Ministry of Justice
　　　　　　　　　　　　　　　　　　NG-Persecutions of Jews

SUMMARY:

　　　A and C) JOEL reports on the spoliation of Jews in Nuernberg
after the Pogrom Night of November 9, 1938. The Jews were forced
by the "Gau Franken" to sell their real-estates for 10% of the
true value. The competent judge of the Amtsgericht of Fuerth,
LEISS, refused energetically, to enter the sales in the "Grund-
buch" (register of real-estates). He regarded the action as illegal
His resistance failed however since the State-Secretary Dr. SCHLEGEL-
BERGER and the President of the District-Court of Nuernberg, HOESCH
stated that the legality of these spolication acts was beyond doubt.

Doc. 17

164

B) JOEL reports how SA-Oberfuehrer KOENIG - with the help of
   "Gauschatzmeister" HOELLERICH and Chief-Prosecuting-Attorney
   DENZLER - earned 70.000.- RM by buying and selling of Jewish
   piece of property, namely the "Fraenkische Dampfziegelwerk
   G.m.b.H. in Forchheim".-

165

Chief Public Prosecutor Dr. Joel

at present Nuernberg,
15 February 1939.

handwritten Rg. 16/2
initial Gu.

Subject: Measures for the aryanization of Jewish
real estate, with particular cooperation
of Notaries Public and the Magistrates
in charge of Land Registry in Nuernberg
and Nuernberg-Fuerth.

I had a thorough conference with the Magistrate
in charge of Land Registry at the Local Court in
Fuerth, Herr Amtsgerichtsrat LEISS, today. Amtsgerichtsrat LEISS reported on his experiences with
entries in the Land Register from the point of view
mentioned above and made roughly the following statement:

After the well-known antisemitic demonstrations
which occured in the Reich on 9 and 10 November 1938,
the Land Registry Office in Fuerth received a telephone call from deputy-Gauleiter HOLZ on the afternoon of 10 November. The call was answered by
clerk of Justice (Justizinspektor) OERTELT. The
Deputy-Gauleiter requested from the Land Registry
an immediate roster of all Jewish landowners in the
district. Later another telephone call came through
in which the person calling introduced himself as
"Streicher's office calling". The second call requested that when the roster of Jewish landowners was
made out the mortgages on each piece of real estate
should be put down. Apart from these calls the
following people appeared in person at the Land Registry Office. Stadtoberamtmann KERN of the town of
Fuerth and later, as a delegate of the party, party-
comrade SANDREUTHER who is a town councillor (Stadtrat) of Fuerth. Both renewed the request which had
been made over the telephone. Amtsgerichtsrat

(page 2 of original)

LEISS informed the presiding judge of the Local
Court, Amtsgerichtsdirektor GREINER, of the requests.
The latter delegated personnel from other sections
and the town council (Stadtrat) of Fuerth assigned
auxiliary clerks for the task. Thereupon the lists
were made out without delay.

166

- 1 -

(page 2 of original, cont'd)

To speed up the work the Treasury Department had temporarily ceded its index-file of Jews to the Land Registry Office.

When the lists were ready some of them were handed over to party-comrade SANDREUTER personally as delegate of the Party, the rest were collected by a girl-secretary of SANDREUTHER's.

On 14 November 1938 Stadtoberamtsmann KERN delivered to the Land Registry Office the first two deeds on sales resulting from the aryanization. In the first of these the town of Fuerth acquired from the Jewish Congregation all its real estate property (synagogue, two cimeteries, administration building, schoolhouse, orphanage and most probably also the Jewish hospital). The legal assessed value of this real estate property amounted to over RM 100.000.-. As purchasing price the amount of RM 100.- was inserted. In the second deed the town of Fuerth acquired from a private Jewish inhabitant, SAALMANN, real estate of a legal assessed value of approximately RM 20.000.-. As purchasing price RM 180.- was entered. These deeds were formally correct. In spite of this Amtsgerichtsrat LEISS refused to make the requisite entry in the Land Register. He held the opinion that in view of the low purchasing price special measures must be taken in the process of aryanization and that he must therefore first report the matter to his superior. Oberamtmann KERN accepted this statement with the reservation

(page 3 of original)

that he would have to inform party-comrade SANDREUTER about it. This conversation took place in the presence of Amtsgerichtsdirektor GREINER between Amtsgerichtsrat LEISS and Oberamtmann KERN.

On 15 November 1938 the town councillor (Ratsherr) Dr. ZEIDLER of Fuerth, in his capacity as representative of the purchasing party, the town of Fuerth, tried to get Amtsgerichtsrat LEISS to register the transaction. Amtsgerichtsrat LEISS was at that time on the point of expressing his scruples in a letter to the presiding judge of the Local Court of

167

(page 3 of original, cont'd)

hand-
written
note:
Enclo-
sure I

Fuerth. He just was engaged on the report dated
15 November 1938, a copy of which is enclosed, addres
to the presiding judge at the Local Court of Fuerth.
Following on this Amtsgerichtsrat LEISS had
another telephone call from party-comrade SAND-
REUTER. SANDREUTER said that he was not approaching
him as Amtsrichter (Judge of Local Court), but
as a party-comrade, and that he had informed the
Gauleitung (Regional board of the Party) about
the matter so that there should be no obstacles
put in its way. Amtsgerichtsrat LEISS again
expressed to party-comrade SANDREUTER the scruples
he had exposed in his letter of 15 November 1938.
Amtsgerichtsrat LEISS read this report to party-
comrade SANDREUTER and later transmitted a copy
of his report to be passed on to the Gauleitung.

Amtsgerichtsdirektor GREINER, who had heard
the conversation between Amtsgerichtsrat LEISS
and Stadtoberamtmann KERN about the question
of the entry, had had an interview with the Landes-
gerichtspraesident (Presiding Judge of the Provincial Court) in the meantime. Amtsgerichtsrat
LEISS transmitted the report of 15 November
1938 to Amtsgerichtsdirektor GREINER, whereupon
Amtsgerichtsdirektor GREINER went again with
this report to see Landgerichtspraesident Dr.
HOESCH in Nuernberg. Shortly after Amtsgerichtsdirektor GREINER had left his office, the Ober-

168

(page 4 of original)

buergermeister (Mayor) and Kreisleiter (party
district leader) Jacob of Fuerth and town councillor
party-comrade SANDREUTER called there. As the Amtsgerichtsdirektor was absent, they were received by
clerk of justice (Justizinspektor) DOERRER. Ober-
buergermeister JACOB is reported to have said to
Justizinspektor DOERRER that the Gauleitung would
make Amtsgerichtsrat LEISS hurry up.

On returning from his interview with Landgerichtspraesident Dr. HOESCH, Amtsgerichtsrat
LEISS declared that the Landgerichtspraesident

- 3 -

(page 4 of original, cont'd)

also had nothing against the legalization of the
deeds. Nevertheless Amtsgerichtsrat LEISS thought
he should ask for another interview with the
Landgerichtspraesident and shortly afterwards went
to Nuernberg for that purpose.

Landgerichtspraesident HOESCH declared that
already two notaries public had remonstrated with
him, since they had scruples about the legalization
of the documents requested by the delegate of the
Party. There could be no doubt, he said, that the
agreements had been made under pressure and that
therefore the deeds gave a wrong impression of
the facts. But he had succeeded in removing these
scruples in a joint discussion. In reply to the
scruples of Amtsgerichtsrat LEISS Landgerichtspraesident HOESCH expressed the opinion that the
question of free will might perhaps be doubtful,
but that, after all, every action in human life
was subject to some special influence. It was
quite clear from this that the Landgerichtspraesident
had no scruples and that he did not wish to get
into trouble with the Gauleitung. Amtsgerichtsrat
LEISS finally declared that he would now start
legalizing the deeds, but that he kept to the
legal interpretation laid down in his report of 15
November 1938, and said that he would issue a report
on the legalization with reference to this conference. Landgerichtspraesident HOESCH,

(page 5 of original)

however, gave him to understand that a written
report was neither desirable nor necessary. Landgerichtspraesident HOESCH fell sick on the morning
after the interview with Amtsgerichtsrat LEISS and
did not come back to the office until some days ago.
So that in the days which ensued Amtsgerichtsrat
LEISS had only to deal once in the matter with
his deputy in office, Landgerichtsirektor GREINER.

In the meantime the aryanization in Fuerth was
handled in the following way: SA-men would pick
up Jews, town councillor party-comrade SANDREUTER

- 4 -

(page 5 of original, cont'd)

and Gaufachgruppenleiter (the leader of the vo-
cational group of the province) of the German
Labor Front (DAF) Nagel would negotiate with them
in the town hall, while the notaries public KEIM
and MAIER were busy in another room of the town hall
where the Jews were soon brought before them.
Sales were effected by entering 10% of the
legal assessed value as the purchasing price while
mortgages were redeemed and the costs had to be paid
by the Jews themselves. Later they proceeded also to
aryanize mortgages, i.e. the Jews received 10%
of the mortgage value as a compensation for the
cession. Subsequent reductions in the purchasing
prices also occurred. This happened in the case
of purchasing contracts which had been drawn up
before 9 November 1938, but which had not yet
been legalized in the Land Register. Even in deeds
which had already been legally entered in the Land
Register such reductions of purchasing prices
occurred.

hand-
written
initial

B!

170

At a further conference with town councillor
SANDREUTER and

(page 6 of original)

Gaufachgruppenleiter NAGEL the question was discussed
as to what importance it would have for the entry
if the tax fees on the notary's deeds were not
paid. Amtsgerichtsrat LEISS declared that the
notary public could, on principle, only submit
the documents to the Land Registry after the tax
fees had been paid, but that this was an affair
which did not concern the magistrate in charge of
Land Registry and which would have to be accounted
for by the notaries public. The two party delegates,
however, told Amtsgerichtsrat LEISS that the
notaries public would be given a general suspension
of this regulation by the competent District Finance Officer. As it has been ascertained, this
suspension by the District Finance Officer was
never given. The conference prompted Amtsgerichtsrat

(page 6 of original, cont'd)

LEISS to suggest a suspension of the Court Fee
Regulations according to which no entries might be
made in the Land Register without pre-payment of
the fees. Landgerichtsdirektor GREINER, the deputy
Landgerichtspraesident, was asked about this
over the telephone by Gaufachgruppenwalter NAGEL.
Some time later Landgerichtsdirektor GREINER
called up Amtsgerichtsrat LEISS on the subject
and declared "he would have to do the whole thing
on his own responsibility, he, GREINER, would back
him in any case."

Another request was made to Amtsgerichtsrat
LEISS which intimated that even the formal pre-
requisites for the entry of notes in the Land
Register no longer existed. The Notary Public Dr.
KEIM pointed out to Amtsgerichtsrat LEISS that
entries would now have to be made in the Public
Land Register also in favor of the future purchaser
who was to be appointed by the Gauleitung, so as
to secure his claim to the transfer of the property.

171

(page 7 of original)

hand-   This must be done also in cases where not all co-
written) proprietors had given their consent to entry as was
remark:) required by the law concerning registration. This
          request prompted Amtsgerichtsrat Leiss to report
Enclo-   again to the Landgerichtspraesident on 21 November
sure II) 1938. Amtsgerichtsdirektor Dr. Greiner brought this
          report back from the Landgerichtspraesident with the
          remark that, if entries had to be made anyhow, the
          report was superfluous. Besides that, if the report
          did have to be submitted, one sentence in it would
          have to be crossed out, viz: "the authorities in charge
          hope that the co-proprietors who reside elsewhere
          will feel concern for the fate of the co-proprietors
          residing here, and will subsequently send them the
          necessary powers of attorney". A copy of this report
          is enclosed. On 26 November 1938 Amtsgerichtsdirektor
          Dr. Greiner declared that not only the Landgerichts-
          praesident but also Secretary of State Dr. Schlegel-
          berger in the Reich Ministry of Justice feel no
          scruples about the desired registration. In spite
172   of this, Amtsgerichtsrat Leiss still asked for
          the report to be submitted as he had referred to
          it in the files of the Land Register. Amtsgerichts-
          rat Dr. Greiner therefore urged him to report on
          these statements he had added to the Land Register
          files, and this he did in his report of 28 November
          1938, a copy of which is enclosed. After these
(hand-   reports Amtgerichtsrat Leiss heard no more of the
written   matter until 21 December 1938. On 21 December 1938
Enclo-   the following decree was issued by the Landgerichts-
sure   praesident to the Amtsgerichtsdirektor (Presiding
III   Judge of the Local Court) in Fuerth-No. 385 E -

                    "In reply to the report of 1 December 1938 I
                    beg to inform Amtsgerichtsrat Leiss as
                    follows:

                1. Directives or instructions concerning the
                    processing of sales of Jewish real estate
                    are not to be expected at present.

                    (page 8 of original)

                2. The magistrate in charge of the Land Register
                    will order the legalization of the deeds or
                    will refuse it.

                3. Such remarks in the files of the Land Register
                    as: "For legal judgment see enclosed copies
                    of the reports of 15 and 21 November 1938"

(page 8 of original cont'd)

and "For legal judgment see statement in
Land Register files Fuerth No. 2200/226"
are inadmissible and will be removed from
the files together with the reports.
The reports of 15 and 21 November 1938 conce
internal office matters of the judicial admi
nistration and will therefore be filed
with the records on internal office affairs
collective files.

By deputy

(Signed): Greiner,
Landgerichtsdirektor

The registrations requested were entered until
Saturday, 3 December 1938, when the matter was
settled. by law through the ordinance on the uti-
lization of Jewish property of 3 December 1938.

On 3 December 1938, at 22:00 hours the deputy
of town councillor Sandreuther, administrative
inspector Rahn, called on Amtsgerichtsrat Leiss
and begged him to see town councillor Sandreuter
without delay. Rahn hinted that legal instructions were to be expected from Berlin and that
Gauinspekteur Ritter also would be present.
Amtsgerichtsrat Leiss met Gauinspekteur Ritter,
town councillor Sandreuter, Gaufachgruppenwalter
Nagel and Gaufachgruppenwalter Wolff in the private
rooms of the innkeeper Sandmann. The gentlemen
had already had a conference with notary public
Dr. Keim and reported that the acceptance of
the numerous sales offers should now be declared.

(page 9 of original)

The Gau Franken (Province of Franconia) of the
NSDAP should be entered as purchasing party.
Amtsgerichtsrat Leiss replied that it hardly
could be done this way as the Gau had no legal
personality, so that Gauleiter Streicher himself
would have to be registered as the purchasing party.
The delegates of the Gau objected to this because
the name of the Gauleiter must not be used.
Amtsgerichtsrat Leiss declared that he would have
to inform the Landgerichtspraesident and the Amtsgerichtsdirektor in case of insistance on the
entry of the Gau. With this the discussion was
closed as regards essentials.

173

- 8 -

(page 9 of original cont'd)

The next morning, Sunday 4 December 1938,
Amtsgerichtsrat Leiss informed Amtsgerichtsdirektor
Greiner about the conference. The notaries public
Maier and Keim of Fuerth had made out four deeds
in the name of the Gau Franconia in the meantime.

Amtsgerichtsdirektor Dr. Greiner, Amtsgerichtsrat Leiss and notary public Dr. Keim now decided
to call on the deputy Landgerichtspraesident in
Nuernberg. On their way to the interview they
visited the magistrate in charge of Land Registration, Oberamtsrichter Daerr in Nuernberg, to see
what the latter had experienced and felt in the
matter. Whilst they were with Oberamtsrichter
Daerr, Gaufachgruppenwalter Wolff appeared and
invited those present to join in a conference
with the deputy Gauleiter Holz. At the conference
with deputy - Gauleiter Holz the following took
part: town councillor Sandreuter, the Gaufachgruppenwalter Wolff and Nagel,   the 3 notaries public,
involved in the aryanization of Jewish real estate
property in Nuernberg, Reinfurt, Keppel and Hussel,

(page 10 of original)

the magistrate in charge of land registration in
Nuernberg, Oberamtsrichter Daerr, the magistrate
in charge of land registration in Fuerth, Amtsgerichtsrat Leiss, Amtsgerichtsdirektors Grueber
of Nuernberg, and Greiner of Fuerth. The Deputy-
Gauleiter Holz and Gaufachgruppenwalter Nagel were
the spokesmen. Quick action was now necessary,
they said, and the entries would have to be made
right away, if possible. The Gau should not be
registered as purchasing party. The objection
of Amtsgerichtsrat Leiss was admitted to be valid,
that if the Gau were entered in the records the
NSDAP would be meant all the same and that therefore further sales would be subject to the
consent of the Reich Treasury Department of the
Party. It was therefore decided to enter deputy-
Gauleiter Holz as quasi-trustee purchaser in the
Land Register so as to enable the Gau to dispose
of the properties and to exclude intervention of
the Reich Treasury Department of the Party. The
reasons given for this were that the Gau Franconia
had its own special merits in the Jewish problem
and that it must therefore receive special rights.
The special tasks of the Gau in town planning and
in connection with the Reichsparteitag (National

- 9 -

(page 10 of original cont'd)

Party Congress) as well as the fact that its
production is weak if it is compared with other
Provinces, and that it has been particularly looted
by the Jews, would justify its acquiring an extraordinary amount of property. After this conference
deputy-Gauleiter Holz was entered in the Land
Register as owner about 40-45 times, in Nuernberg
about 450 times.

After the decree of the Deputy General for
the Four Year Plan had taken legal effect on
Tuesday, 6 December, 1938, and aryanization was made
subject to the consent of the Regierungspraesident
(District President) no further entries were made.

(Signature): Dr. JOEL

175

- 10 -

(page 11 of original)

Copy of a copy.   (Handwritten:)   I

Lower Court Fuerth in Bavaria

 -Land Registry -

Herr

Amtsgerichtsdirektor,

Fuerth / Bavaria.

After the events of 9 November 1938 the Land Registry, by order of.
the Gauleitung and the commissioner (town councillor party-comrade
Sandreuther) entrusted by the party to carry through aryanization
within the township of Fuerth, has made copies of the Land Register
of real estate in possession of Jewish owners. The excerpts will be
used by the competent authorities as basic material in the nego-
tations with Jewish owners.

On 14 November 1938 the first two public notary contracts were
submitted, which are to be considered the result of the latest
aryanization measures. In the near future, a great number of similar
contracts must be expected. This fact implies a number of problems
for the Land Registry, which appear to be of basic importance in
different respects and may cause, in my opinion, the issue of regulations by the legislative authorities. I therefore take the
liberty of making the following statements:

The contracts submitted have the outward form of purchasing
contracts with conveyance. In view of their fixed purchasing
prices and of the accompanying circumstances, their essential
nature, is however, that of a forced expropriation, carried through
either without or only with slight compensation. The legal judgment
of these contracts can, of course, not be made on common civil
law principles, the contracts being legal acts which, as a result
of the sovereignty of the Party, are not subject to control by
regular authorities.

As a precaution, I am, therefore, inquiring whether any regulations of
the competent authorities concerning the handling of those contracts may be expected.

(page 12 of original)

The Reich might e.g. claim the difference between the fixed purchasing price and the standard price.

Furthermore, I beg you to inform me, whether regulations may be
expected which clarify the extent and subjects of the legal
control of the Judge of the Land Registry, as far as the above
mentioned contracts are concerned.

-11-

(page 12 of original continued)

For the time being, I shall not legalize the two submitted contracts, nor ⁿ those to be expected in future, until I receive the requested information.

Fuerth, 15 November 1938

(signature) Leiss

Amtsgerichtsrat.

177

(page 13 of original)

<u>copy of a copy</u>   II

To

the Landgerichtspraesident

<u>in Nuernberg.</u>

Referring to my inquiry addressed in the course of the morning
of 15 November 1938 to the Amtsgerichtsdirektor in Fuerth, and to
my conference on this matter with the Landgerichtspraesident in
the afternoon of the same day, I beg to inform you, that the Land
Registry at Fuerth in Bavaria, after having made further excerpts
of the Land Register, will now start with the legalization of
these instruments in the Land Register.

Further instruments have been received, in which Jewish landowners
engage themselves to transfer their property rights in their real
estate to a purchaser to be later appointed by the Gauleitung
Franconia of the NSDAP. Preliminary entries are supposed to be
made in the Land Register to secure the claims of the future
purchaser.

178

The notarial instruments are being submitted for legalization
without payment of stamp duty. According to the contents of the
instruments, the total costs will be paid by the future purchasers.
The land Registry, in accordance with the declaration of the
Deputy-Landgerichtspraesident given by telephone on 7 November
1938, will make advance payment of the stamp duty a prerequisite for
the entry of the claims.

Notary public Dr. Keim in Fuerth, Bavaria, and public notary inspector
Hoffmann acting with notary public Dr. Maier in Fuerth, Bavaria,
have announced that even instruments will be submitted for preliminary entry, which do not contain the consent of all Jewish co-owners
in the case of existing co-ownership. Allegedly these are cases
in which the co-owners are living abroad or out of town and therefore the co-owners accessible in Fuerth did not produce the corresponding powers of attorney.

(page 14 of original)

It is hoped by the appropriate authorities, that the co-owners
abroad will send the corresponding powers of attorney later
to the co-owners here simply out of concern for their fate.
The preliminary entries shall be made now and the submission of
the powers of attorney or the consent shall not be waited for.

In accordance with my opinion as contained in the written inquiry of
15 November 1938 mentioned above, I shall make these preliminary
entries, too. Should there be any doubts in this matter, I beg you
to inform me accordingly. The legalization of the new aryanizing
contracts in the Land Register as resulting from the events of
9/10 November 1938 constitutes an uncontrollable political administrative measure for the handling of which I consider myself
bound to the directives of the superior judicial administrative
authorities.

(signature:) Leiss.
Amtsgerichtsrat.

-13-

(page 15 of original)

copy of a copy.

Lower Court—Land Registry   Fuerth, Bavaria, 28 Nov. 1938

To the

Amtsgerichtsdirektor

in Fuerth, Bavaria.

In accordance with your directives I hereby inform you in writing,
that I made a statement concerning the new aryanization contracts
mentioned in my reports of 15 and 21 November 1938, in respect
to the legal status of these contracts, adding to the records a
memorandum note mentioning the two reports when legalizing the
entries in the Land Register.

The memorandum note to the first contract literally reads as
follows:"For the interpretation of the legal status see enclosed
copies of reports of 15 and 21 November 1938." With the further
contracts the note reads: " For the interpretation of legal status
see statement in Land Register record, file No. 2200/226."

Although it has been made clear through verbal information on
26 November 1938 that, in accordance with your view and that of the
Landgerichtspraesident, State Secretary Schlegelberger of the Reich
Ministry of Justice, too, has no scruples against the legalization
of the instruments by the Land Registry, and that the activities of
the Land Registry Fuerth are therefore approved by the competent
authorities, I yet think it advisable to retain the above mentioned statement in regard to the rest of the documents as well. By my comment on the
legal interpretation as given in the above mentioned reports of
15 and 21 November 1938, it is made clear that a potential reviewing
of these contracts by the courts cannot be made under application
of common civil law (e.g. Articles 123, 124, Civil Code) which,
for instance, in case of subsequent contestation of these contracts
by Jewish owners after their emigration and after their possible
naturalization in foreign countries, might be desirable in the interests
of legal security,

                        (signature) Leis.
                        Amtsgerichtsrat.

179

(page 16 of original)

Chief Public Prosecutor Dr. Joël   at present Nuernberg, 16 Feb. 1939

117 So.

Subject: Measures for the aryanization of Jewish real estate
        property at Nuernberg.
        - relative to my report of 15 February 1939.

In the measures for the aryanization of Jewish real estate property
the Justizraete Keppel, H u s s e l and R e i n f u r t have
collaborated as notaries public in Nuernberg. In Fuerth the councillors
of Justice Dr. K e i m and M e y e r, or as deputy of the latter,
Dr. P a b s t were active.

As judges of the Land Registry Oberamtsrichter Daerr and Amtsgerichtsrat Dr. P e t s c h n e r have been assigned to this task at
Nuernberg, I discussed the matter today. The judges and the notaries
public have the intention of submitting their opinion in writing
at their earliest convenience.

180

(signature)   Dr. Joël.

(page 17 of original)

Chief Public Prosecutor Dr. Joël.   at present Nuernberg,
                                          16 Feb 1939.

                    R e p o r t

Re: Purchase and resale of the Fraenkische Ziegelwarke (Franconian
    brick yard) at Forchheim by SA-Oberfuehrer K o e n i g/

Participation of the Chief Public Prosecutor, Gaurechtsamtsleiter
(Chief of the Provincial Party Law Office) D e n z l e r.

As may be seen from the records of the Supreme Party Court in the
case against the adjutant of Gauleiter Streicher, SA-Oberfuehrer
K o e n i g, - II. Section D 42 - Franconia 1937 - and from the
files of Police Headquarters Nuernberg as well as of the Secret
State Police Office in Berlin - II E 5124-38 g - a date had been
set on 23 July 1937 for compulsory auction of the Forchheimer
Dampfziegelwerke, G.m.b.H. at Forchheim, Upper Franconia, before
the Lower Court at Forchheim. The acting judge was Assessor Anton
E g g e r t. Assessor E g g e r t had inspected the plant on the
day before the auction. On this occasion he met Gauschatzmeister
(Provincial Treasurer of the Party) H o e l l e r i c h who
showed particular interest. In the conversation the Assessor learned
that one of Hoellerich's acquaintances wanted to acquire the plant
in the auction.

On the date fixed SA-Oberfuehrer Koenig presented himself in uniform
as a bidding party. He was accompanied by Gauschatzmeister Hoellerich
- who was also in uniform - and Gaurechtsamtsleiter, personal legal
advisor and friend of Koenig, Chief Public Prosecutor Denzler (in
plain clothes). There was a large crowd in the visitor's room.
Only 4 bids were made i.e. one by the Municipal Savings bank of
Forchheim, 118.000.-- RM, the second by the SA-Oberfuehrer Koenig,
120.000.-- RM, the third by the manager of the Fränkische Gewerbe-
bank and

                 (page 18 of original)

liquidator of the Hausbesitzerbank at Nuernberg, Otto Kuhr, personally,
145.000.-- RM, and the last by Oberfuehrer Koenig 147.000.-- RM.
The property was given to Koenig. Bank Manager Kuhr had come to an
agreement on the last bid with SA-Oberfuehrer Koenig during the
compulsory auction.

It is said that other would-be purchasers felt intimidated by the
presence of Koenig, as well as of the Gauschatzmeister and of the
Chief Public Prosecutor and Gaurechtsamtsleiter accompanying him,
so much, so that Koenig, after his agreement with Bank Manager Kuhr,
could purchase the plant at the price of 147,000 RM in the auction.

Koenig had raised the money in the following manner:

    1.) 1100.000.-- RM mortage from the Bayrische Hypotheken- &
                       Wechselbank
    2.)   40.000.-- RM gift of the Gauleiter
    3.)   30.000.-- RM loan of town councillor Schneider.

181

(page 18 of original continued)

Since the plant yielded bo profit and suffered even losses, it
was obvious that its re-sale would be attemted as soon as
possible. It is said that Gaurechtsamtsleiter Otto Denzler has
been active in this business, constantly advising and cooperating
without appearing publicly, besides Gauschatzmeister Hoellerich.
There re-sale was brought in the following way: -

In Eltersdorf near Erlangen there is a clay works which belonged to
the Jew K i r s c h b a u m and was estimated at about 650.000.—RM
in value. The civilian engineer August Meyer, Nuernberg, Plattenstr.
55 had agreed upon a purchasing price of 550.000.— RM with the Jew
in case of immediate purchase. A preliminary contract made out by
the notary public had been submitted to the Chamber of Industry
and Commerce and the Gauwirtschaftsberater with the request for
their consent. Gauwirtschaftsberater (Provincial Economic Advisor)
Strobl told Meyer that he could only give his consent to the
purchase, if Meyer simultaneously bought the Fraenkisches Ziegelwerk at Forchheim at a price of 300,000.— RM.

In spite of the bad business conditions of the Forchheimer .
Ziegelwerke, and in spite of being aware of the fact, that the
Eltersdorfer Clay Plant had no economic relation whatever with
it, the Gauwirtschaftsberater

(page 19 of original)

made it a condition for his consent to the sale, that the Forchheimer Ziegelwerk should be purchased together with it.

On 23 May Meyer was summoned to appear at the Gayhaus (Provincial
Party Building) before Gauschatzmeister Hoellerich, who told him
the same story as Strobl and promised him business orders from
the Party in case of purchase. In the beginning Meyer replied in
the negative, but asked, on 9 June 1938, the Deputy Gauwirtschaftsberater (Provincial Economic Advisor) Dr. Beckh, whether he
would obtain the permit to purchase the Eltersdorf Clay Works.
He was told to wait for the return of the Gauwirtschaftsberater and
that the Eltersdorf Clay Works were only for sale together with
the Forchheim Brick Yard.

On 14 June 1938 Hoellerich called Meyer up by telephone and
told him that the Gauleitung was interested in his individually
purchasing the Forchheim brick yard, although there were still 7
or 8 candidates for the deal. The Jew Kirschbaum would be put
under pressure by the Gauleitung to reduce the price, so as to
make the purchase of the Forchheim brickyard cheaper for Meyer.
The valuator Pabst, formerly owner of the Forchheim brickyard,
told the banking advisor of Meyer that Gauschatzmeister Hoellerich
had given him the same information. At first Meyer thought of
rejecting the deal entirely, but later made the following offer
through the assistant field manager of the Commerz & Privatbank
A.G. in Nuernberg, so as not to incur the Party's displeasure:

Meyer would take shares up to 100,000.— RM if an expert business
man could be found, who would purchase the Forchheim brickyard
for 275.000.— RM.

On 17 June 1938 the son of the Jew Kirschbaum was summoned to
appear before the legal advisor of the chamber of Industry and
Commerce Dr. Hofmann who told him that the purchasing price
of 558.000.— RM agreed upon with Meyer was too high. It would

182

-17-

(page 19 of original continued)

have to be reduced to 496.000.— RM. In spite

(page 20 of original)

of a stubborn refusal, the sale was made at 496,000.— RM.

In respect to the Sale of the Franconian brickyard at Forchheim,
it was agreed upon that an interested engineer, Kegelmann, from
Aachen in Baden, would purchase the brickyard together with
Meyer, who would take 100,000.— RM in shares. Only after this
was the sale of the clay works Eltersdorf "allowed".
After deduction of the 100,000 RM mortgage of the Bayrische
Hypotheken & Wechselbank K o e n i g received 175,000.— RM
in cash and 30,000.— RM for material in stock. The total
ammount of 205,000.— RM was remitted to the Coburg Savings
Bank at Nuernberg. The net provit for Koenig, in this "deal"
was approximately 75,000.— RM.

Later Koenig still made Bank Manager Kuhr pay 7000.— RM to
himself, since in the purchase price agreed upon in the auction,
it allegedly had not been taken into account, that litigations
on stock reserves had arisen and law-suits with neighbours were
pending.

As mentioned above, Chief Public Prosecutor Denzler is said to
have collaborated in all phases of this deal as a close advisor
of Koenig.

(signature) Dr. Joel

183

CERTIFICATE OF TRANSLATION
OF DOCUMENT No. NG-616

Nuernberg, 28 February 1947

I, Helga Lund, Mil. Entry Permit 026027, herewith certify that I
am thoroughly conversant with the English and German languages,
and that the above is a true and correct translation of the
document no. NG-616.

HELGA LUND
Mil. Entry Permit 026027

LEGAL ADVISER

No. 511

Subject: German Decree of December 14, 1938,
Eliminating Jewish Plant Managers -
Embassy's Note of December 29 to
German Foreign Office.

ADVISER ON POLITICAL RELATIONS
MR JOHN
JAN 17 1939
DEPARTMENT OF STATE

RECEIVED
DEPARTMENT OF STATE
1959 JAN 14 AM 11 00

Doc. 18

184

DEPARTMENT OF STATE
ASSISTANT SECRETARY
JAN 18 1939
A-M/C

The Honorable

The Secretary of State,

Washington.

Sir:

With reference to the Embassy's telegram No. 764
of December 29   1 p.m., I have the honor to enclose a
translation of a German decree of December 14, 1938,
which provides in general for the elimination of Jews
as managers of plants.   There is also enclosed a copy

2.   of the Embassy's note of December 29 addressed to the
German Foreign Office, which requests assurances that
this decree will not be applied to American citizens.

Respectfully yours,

Prentiss Gilbert
Chargé d'Affaires ad interim

Enclosures:
    1. Translation of
       Decree;
    2. From Embassy to
       Foreign Office,
       December 29, 1938.
350
JWR:AC

Copy to Consulate General, Berlin.

Translation
from
REICHSGESETZBLATT, Part I, No. 223
December 23, 1938.

Second Decree
for the execution of the Decree
For Excluding Jews from German
Economic Life

Of December 14, 1938.

On the basis of Section 4 of the Decree For Excluding
The Jews From German Economic Life of November 12, 1938
(REICHSGESETZBLATT Part I, p..1580) it is decreed:

Section 1

In plants the principal of which is a Jew, the Reich
Labor Trustee has to appoint a manager (Betriebsführer)
in the sense of the Law For Regulating National Labor (AOG)
of January 20, 1934 (REICHSGESETZBLATT Part I p. 45) and of
the Law For Regulating Labor In Public Administrations and
Plants (AOGÖ) of March 23, 1934 (REICHSGESETZBLATT Part I
p. 220) who fulfills the premises in regard to race (Blut)
for acquiring Reich citizenship.   The Reich Labor Trustee
may issue regulations concerning the shaping of relations
between the manager and the principal.

If a manager appointed in accordance with Section 1
proves materially or personally unsuited, the Reich Labor
Trustee may recall him.

Section 2

(1) The regulations of Section 1 also apply to Jews
who, as legal representatives of juridical persons and
groups of persons (Personengesamtheiten), are managers

in

185

in accordance with Section 3 AOG.

(2) In these cases the Reich Labor Trustee may refrain from appointing new managers if, in addition to
the Jews, other persons are managers as legal representatives and an orderly social-political management of the
plant is thus guaranteed.

Section 3

From January 1, 1939, on Jews may also no longer be
acting managers.

Section 4

If the premises of Sections 1 and 2 of this Decree
obtain in a plant, the principal must without delay inform
the Reich Labor Trustee to this effect.

186

Section 5

An indemnification is not granted for personal or
economic disadvantages which arise from the carrying out
of this decree.   The measures adopted on the basis of
this decree by the Reich Labor Trustee do not establish
liability on the part of the Reich.

Section 6

The Reich Labor Trustee may permit exceptions from
the regulations of this decree.

Berlin, December 14, 1938.

The Reich Minister of Economics
Brinkmann, Acting

The Reich Minister of Labor
Dr. Krohn, Acting

The Reich Minister of the Interior
Pfundtner, Acting.

HCF

COPY

No. 274

    The Embassy of the United States of America has the
honor to advise the Ministry for Foreign Affairs that its
attention has been drawn to a German decree of December
14, 1938, entitled "Second Decree for the Execution of the
Decree excluding Jews from German Economic Life", which
was published in REICHSGESETZBLATT I, No. 223 of December
23, 1938.

    By its terms, this decree would appear to exclude
Jews from acting as plant managers (Betriebsführer) at
least in a number of cases.   It is noted, however, that
according to Section 6 of the decree, the Reich Labor
Trustee is authorized to allow exceptions to the regulations established therein.

    The Embassy is confident that in the application of
this decree of December 14, 1938, American citizens will
be exempted from its provisions, and would appreciate
the early assurances of the Ministry for Foreign Affairs
to this effect.

                    Berlin, December 29, 1938.

187

To the
    Ministry for Foreign Affairs,
        Berlin.

AC

DOCUMENT FILE

NOTE

Doc. 19

188

REGARDING: Statute modifying existing rent laws for purpose of separating
the Jews from the "Aryans" in apartment houses. Copy of the
REICHSGESETZBLATT of May 4 containing the-. Provisions and
purpose of the law.

862.4016/2115

fp

No. 836   Berlin, May 11, 1939

          Subject: Legislation Facilitating the
                    Eviction of Jewish Tenants.

The Honorable

     The Secretary of State,

          Washington.

Sir:

1/
2/   I have the honor to transmit herewith a copy,
and translation of REICHSGESETZBLATT, Part I, No.84,
of May 4, 1939, containing a statute which modifies
existing rent laws for the purpose of separating
Jews from "Aryans" in apartment houses.

          The statute in question does not specifically
compel Jews to vacate houses owned by "Aryans" nor
does it, vice versa, compel "Aryans" to leave houses
owned and inhabited by Jews, but the intent thereof
is rather to deprive Jews of the right of protection
against sudden denunciation of rent contracts in order to permit "Aryan" householders summarily to cancel their contracts and evict Jewish tenants. At

                                             the

189

the same time it is provided that a lessor can only
denounce a rent contract with a Jew if he (the lessor)
is furnished with a certificate by the municipal or
communal authorities that some other quarters are
available for the Jew in a Jewish-owned house. In
this connection, rather extraordinary powers are
vouchsafed the local authorities to enable them to
find and make free alternative quarters for Jews.
These authorities may compel Jewish householders, or
Jewish tenants in a Jewish-owned house, to register
with them vacant rooms, or space which they would not
seem to require for their own needs. The latter may
then be forced, even against their will, to lease
these quarters to other Jews who are liable to eviction from "Aryan" houses. The local authorities may
draw up the terms of these involuntary contracts and
collect a fee for this service. It is provided that
the law may be applied in Austria and the Sudetenland
with necessary emendations.

The purpose of the law is, in short, to effect
the widest possible withdrawal of Jews to houses
owned by Jews and largely inhabited by Jews. In view
of the current housing shortage in most German cities
this will not be an easy matter to accomplish. This
difficulty will in part be circumvented, however, by
the solution indicated in a DEUTSCHES NACHRICHTEN BÜRO
report of May 4, which points out that there are many
wealthy Jews who occupy apartments and villas too
large for their own needs; this report comments that
it is only natural, as the new law so provides, that

they

they should be forced to rent quarters to other Jews,
whose dwellings in turn will be made available to de-
serving German "Aryans."

Under the terms of the law, the definition of a
Jew is that laid down in the Nuremberg racial legislation of September 15, 1935, namely, a person who
has three or more Jewish grandparents or belongs to
the Jewish faith. In the case of mixed marriages,
the provisions will not be applied if only the wife
is Jewish. On the other hand, if the husband is a
Jew and there are no children by the marriage, the
law becomes applicable irrespective of the fact whether the husband or the wife is the lessor or lessee of
a dwelling. In general, a business undertaking defined as Jewish in accordance with the Third Decree
to the Reich Citizenship Law of June 14, 1938 (see
Embassy's despatch No. 197 of June 23, 1938), is to
receive the same treatment as a Jewish private individual.

The law entered into effect the day following
promulgation, that is, on May 6, and apparently cancellation of such rent contracts as come into question may be made from that date, provided that, as
mentioned before, the municipal authorities certify
that other quarters are available. Apparently the
premises are to be vacated as soon as possible there-
after, but in certain cases it is provided that a delay may be granted if a certificate can be obtained
from the local authorities that there are difficul-
ties in the way of a Jew's moving into other quar-

ters

191

tars, or if immediate removal would do "serious damage to the health of one of the parties affected."

As first mentioned above, the law does not compel "Aryan" householders to evict Jews. That pressure from the Party may be brought to bear upon them
to do so is indicated, however, in an article appearing in the FRANKFURTER ZEITUNG of May 10 which reports
that the Reich Ministers of the Interior and of Labor
have issued directive regulations to the local authorities that the cell and block leaders of the National
Socialist Party are to be asked to assist in drawing
up lists of "Aryan" dwellings inhabited by Jews, as
well as of the extra rooms in other Jewish houses which
might in turn be allotted to these Jews. While assert-
ing that a "community of dwelling" (Wohngemeinschaft)
is impossible between Jews and "Aryans," the FRANKFUR-
TER ZEITUNG article denies that the authorities have
any intention of building up "undesirable ghetto districts." It points out that Jews are free to make
among themselves voluntary arrangements for the leas-
ing of premises.

Inasmuch as no exception is specifically provided, the law apparently applies in principle to foreign
Jews. On the other hand, according to the report of
the FRANKFURTER ZEITUNG, the directive regulations
issued by the Ministers of the Interior and Labor provide that before issuing a certificate that alternative quarters are available for foreign Jews living

in

in German "Aryan" houses, the local authorities
must first consult with the Minister of Labor. The
same provision applies also in cases where the local
authorities might wish to establish evicted German
Jews in the quarters of foreign Jews.

Respectfully yours,

Alexander Kirk
Chargé d'Affaires ad interim.

Enclosure:
1. Copy of REICHSGESETZBLATT.
2. Translation of law of April 30,
   1939, contained therein.

800

JDB:KM

193

Enclosure No. 2 to despatch
No. 836 of May 11, 1939, from
American Embassy, Berlin.

Translation
from
REICHSGESETZBLATT, Part I, No. 84
May 4, 1939.

Law
governing the relationship between landlords and tenants
involving Jews.

Of April 30, 1939.

The Reich Government has passed the following
law, which is promulgated herewith:

Section 1

Relaxation of Protection for Tenants

A Jew cannot invoke the legal protection provided for tenants if the lessor, when giving notice, can
prove by a certificate of the municipal authority that
some other quarters are available to the lessee after
the termination of the relationship between the landlord and the tenant.   This does not apply if the
lessor is likewise a Jew.

Section 2

Premature Notice

If only one party to the contract is a Jew, a
lease may be terminated at any time upon legal notice
being given by the other, even if the lease was concluded for a definite time or if a time-limit for
giving notice longer than the legal one was agreed upon.   However, the lessor can only give notice for a

shorter

shorter time than that legally permissible under the lease if when giving notice he can prove by a certificate of the municipal authority that some other quarters are available to the lessee after termination of the relationship between the landlord and tenant.

Section 3

Sublessees

Jews are only permitted to conclude subleases with Jews.   It is not necessary to have the permission of the lessor if he is likewise a Jew.

Section 4

Living Quarters

(1) A Jew living in quarters in his capacity as owner thereof, or by virtue of a right of usufruct, or which he has rented from a Jew, must accommodate Jews as lessees or sublessees at the request of the municipal authority. If the conclusion of the necessary lease is refused, the municipal authority can decree that a lease with the text it stipulates shall be considered as agreed upon. The amount of compensation for making available such quarters and a possible extra subletting charge is stipulated by the municipal authority in concurrence with the competent price authority, unless it is a price authority itself.

(2) The municipality can charge fees for arranging leases and subleases.

(3) A

195

(3) A relationship between landlord and tenant
as per Par. 1 can only be terminated by the lessor or
sublessor with the permission of the municipal authority.

Section 5

Re-leasing

Only with the permission of the municipal authority may Jews re-lease quarters that have become vacant.
The provisions in Section 4 apply to such quarters mutatis mutandis.

Section 6

Effect of Cessation of Administrative Authority

In so far as application of Sections 1 to 5 is con-
tingent upon the lessor being a Jew, the owner of the
property or the person entitled to usufruct thereof is
deemed the lessor even if he did not conclude or cannot
conclude the lease himself due to the fact that his administrative authority has ceased to exist.

Section 7

Mixed Marriages

While the application of this law depends on whether the lessor or lessee is a Jew, the following provisions apply in case of a lessor's or lessee's mixed
marriage:

1. The provisions must/be applied if the wife
   is a Jewess.
   The same applies if there are children by
   the marriage, even if the marriage no longer
   exists.

                                        2. If

- 4 -

2. If the husband is a Jew and there are no
children by the marriage, the provisions
are to be applied without consideration as
to whether the husband or the wife is a less-
or or lessee.

3. Children who are deemed Jews are left out of
consideration.

Section 8

Change in the Right of Disposal

(1) If the right of disposal (property or usufruct) of real estate is transferred from a Jew to a
non-Jew after this law becomes effective, the provisions of this law remain applicable just as they were
prior to the transfer, but premature notice (Section 2)
is precluded. This applies also in case of another
change in the right of disposal.

(2) The provision in Par. 1 does not include
quarters which the party having the right of disposal
intends to use himself or the use of which the municipal authority has renounced. As proof of such renun-
ciation a certificate of the municipal authority suf-
fices.

Section 9

Time-Limit for Vacating

(1) If a Jew is condemned to vacate on the basis
of the provisions of this law, a time-limit for vacating may only be granted him if he proves by a certificate of the municipal authority that there are diffi-

culties

197

culties in the way of his moving into other quarters or if immediate removal cannot be carried out without serious damage to the health of one of the parties affected. The time-limit for vacating may be prolonged under the same conditions.

(2) The provision in Par. 1 must be applied _mutatis mutandis_, unless the vacating party himself gave notice, if the obligation to vacate is not pronounced by a court decision or if the conditions for granting a time-limit for vacating do not occur until after announcement of the court decision. Upon application of the party liable to vacate, the competent Lower Court decides as to the granting of the time-limit. If a time-limit is granted and if there is no enforceable court decree to vacate, the decision must embody the order that the quarters must be vacated after the expiration of the time-limit; this decision is tantamount to an enforceable court decree to vacate (_vollstreckbares Räumungsurteil_).

(3) Immediate action against the decision by which a time-limit to vacate is refused can be entered even if a decision is contested only because of refusal of a time-limit.

(4) Until the quarters are vacated the former parties to the contract have the same rights and duties they had prior to the termination of the relationship between the landlord and the tenant.

(B) In

- 6 -

(5) In the procedure as per Par. 3 the same
court and lawyers' fees are charged as in the procedure involving applications for temporary suspension of execution. Section 10 Par. 1 of the Law
governing court costs applies *mutatis mutandis* to
fixing the costs of litigation.

Section 10

Definitions

(1) Who is a Jew is decided in accordance with
Section 5 of the First Decree to the Reich Citizen
Law of November 14, 1935 (RGB I page 1333).

(2) Except in applying Section 9, a Jewish undertaking in the meaning of Article I of the Third Decree
to the Reich Citizen Law of June 14, 1938 (RGB I page
627) is on a par with a Jew. A cessation of the conditions under which an undertaking is deemed Jewish
must also be regarded as a change in the right of
disposal in the meaning of Section 8.

Section 11

Treatment of Pending Lawsuits involving
Cancellation of Leases

(1) If, at the time this law becomes effective,
is
a lawsuit pending against a Jew or the husband or
wife of a Jew, involving the cancellation of a lease,
the court must suspend the proceedings, upon application of the plaintiff, in order to give him an oppor-
tunity to give notice according to the provisions of

this

199

this law.   If the plaintiff terminates the relationship, he can petition to have the proceedings
instituted and change from the action for cancellation to the action for vacating. If the litigation
is settled by the lessee moving out or accepting the
demand to vacate (Räumungsanspruch), the court costs
arising from the litigation involving cancellation must
be canceled; extra-judicial costs must be borne by the
lessee.

(2) If the plaintiff withdraws the action for
cancellation, the costs of the court must be canceled
and the extrajudicial costs balanced against each
other.

Section 12
General Obligation to Register

(1) The municipal authority may issue orders
governing the registration of quarters which can be
rented to Jews or which can be claimed for housing
Jews in accordance with the provisions of this law.

(2) Anyone who deliberately or by neglect fails
to see to the prescribed registration or does not do
so in time will be punished by a fine not exceeding
150 reichsmarks or by imprisonment.

Section 13
Claims to Indemnity Precluded

Claims to indemnification against the municipality cannot be deduced from orders of the municipal
authority which are based on the provisions of this
law.

Section 14

Section 14

Reservation, Empowerment

(1) The application of this law in the State of Austria and in the Sudeten German areas remains reserved.

(2) The Reich Minister of Justice and the Reich Minister of Labor are empowered, in concurrence with the Reich Minister of the Interior, to issue regulations for carrying out and supplementing this law and for introducing corresponding regulations in the State of Austria and in the Sudeten German areas.

Berlin, April 30, 1939.

The Führer and Reich Chancelor
Adolf Hitler

The Reich Minister of Justice
Dr. Gürtner

The Reich Minister of Labor
Dr. Krohn, Acting

The Deputy of the Führer
R. Hess

The Reich Minister of the Interior
Frick

201

AC:EM

NO. 11

AMERICAN CONSULATE GENERAL

Berlin, Germany, June 6, 1939.

SUBJECT: Jews Excluded from the Travel Agency
Business.

THE HONORABLE

THE SECRETARY OF STATE,

WASHINGTON.

SIR:

Doc. 20

202

With reference to the Embassy's despatch No.
246 of July 16, 1938, transmitting a series of
reports, one of which dealt with the Reich law of
July 6, 1938, EXCLUDING JEWS FROM CERTAIN TRADES
AND FROM ACCESS TO HEALTH RESORTS, I have the honor
to inform the Department that a decree dated May 8,
1939, has now been promulgated which excludes Jews
from the travel agency business. Article 2 permits
the Reich Minister of Economic Affairs to make
exception to the prohibition in individual cases.
For the purposes of this decree, the definition of
a Jew is that laid down pursuant to the Nuremberg
racial legislation of September 15, 1935, namely,
a person who has three or more Jewish grandparents
or belongs to the Jewish faith.

There

1/ 2/   There are enclosed a copy and a translation of
the decree which was promulgated in the <u>Reichsgesetz-</u>
<u>blatt</u>, Part I, No. 88, of May 11, 1939, and which is
entitled "Second Decree for the Execution of the Law
Relating to the Business of Travel Agencies."

                                    Respectfully yours,

                                    Raymond H. Geist
                                    American Consul

Enclosures:
    1. Copy of decree of May 11, 1939.
    2. Translation of above decree.

To the Department in quintuplicate.

                                                        203

804.4
CJW/g

Enclosure No. 1 to Despatch No. ⸗ᵢₒf June 6, 1939, from
Consul Raymond H. Geist, Berlin, Germany, on the subject of
JEWS EXCLUDED FROM THE TRAVEL AGENCY BUSINESS.

                                    Source: Reichsgesetzblatt,
                                            Part I, May 11, 1939,
                                            p. 895.

                            COPY

        Zweite Verordnung zur Durchführung des Gesetzes über die
                    Ausübung der Reisevermittlung*

                    Vom 8. Mai 1939.

        Auf Grund des § 3 des Gesetzes über die Ausübung
der Reisevermittlung vom 26. Januar 1937 (Reichsgesetzbl.
I S. 31) wird verordnet:

                            § 1

        Juden (§ 5 der Ersten Verordnung zum Reichsbürger-
gesetz vom 14. November 1935 - Reichsgesetzbl. I S. 1333)
ist vom 1. Juni 1939 ab die gewerbsmässige Ausübung der
Reisevermittlung untersagt.

                            § 2

        Der Reichswirtschaftsminister kann in Einzelfällen
Ausnahmen von den Bestimmungen dieser Verordnung zulassen.

Berlin, den 8. Mai 1939.

                            Der Reichswirtschaftsminister

                                In Vertretung

                                Dr. Landfried

_____

* Betrifft nicht die Ostmark und die sudetendeutschen
  Gebiete.

Enclosure No. 2 to Despatch No.   of June 6, 1939, from
Consul Raymond H. Geist, Berlin, Germany, on the subject of
JEWS EXCLUDED FROM THE TRAVEL AGENCY BUSINESS.

Source: Reichsgesetzblatt,
Part I, May 11, 1939,
p. 895.

TRANSLATION

Second Decree for the Execution of the Law relating to the Business of Travel Agencies*

May 8, 1939.

On the basis of Art. 3 of the Law relating to the
Business of Travel Agencies, January 26, 1938 (Reichsgesetzblatt, Part I, p. 31), the following is decreed:

Article 1

Jews (Art. 5 of the First Decree under the Reich
Citizenship Law, November 14, 1935--Reichsgesetzblatt,
Part I, p. 1333) are forbidden to engage in the travel
agency business on or after June 1, 1939.

Article 2

The Reich Minister of Economic Affairs may in individual cases permit exceptions to the provisions of this
Decree.

Berlin, May 8, 1939.

The Reich Minister of Economic Affairs

By: Dr. Landfried

205

---

* Does not affect Austria or the Sudeten German areas.

Trans.: PNT

CROSS-REFERENCE FILE

NOTE

SUBJECT   Race problems- Germany. Copy of two decrees extending
legislation facilitating the eviction of Jewish tenants,
to Austria and the Sudetenland.

Doc. 21

206

For the original paper from which reference is taken

See ____Despatch #939_____
(Despatch, telegram, instruction, letter, etc.)

Dated ____June 6, 1939____   From| Berlin (Geist)
                              To |

File No. ____862.502/84_____

No.   ꞏꞏꞏꞏ

QUINTUPLICATE

AMERICAN CONSULATE GENERAL,

Berlin, Germany, June 6, 1939.

SUBJECT: Legislation facilitating the Eviction of
          Jewish Tenants extended to Austria and
          the Sudetenland.

THE HONORABLE

    THE SECRETARY OF STATE,

          WASHINGTON.

SIR:

          With reference to the Embassy's despatch No.
836 of May 11, 1939, transmitting a copy and a
translation of the Reich law of April 30, 1939,
Governing the Relationship between Landlords and
Tenants involving Jews, I have the honor to report
that the provisions of that law have now been
adapted and extended to Austria and the Sudetenland
by two decrees both dated May 10, 1939, and promulgated
in the Reichsgesetzblatt, Part I, No. 90, of May 13,
1939.

          This action was taken in compliance with
Section 14 of the law which in part provides that
"the Reich Minister of Justice and the Reich Minister
of Labor are empowered in concurrence with the Reich
Minister of the Interior to issue regulations for
carrying out and supplementing this law and for
introducing corresponding regulations in the State
of Austria and in the Sudeten German area".

                                    Copies

1/

Copies of the decrees mentioned above, as
published in the Reichsgesetzblatt, are enclosed.

Respectfully yours,

Raymond H. Geist
American Consul

Enclosure:
Copies of two decrees
dated May 13, 1939.

204.4

GJW/G

A true copy of
the signed orig-
inal.

Reichsgesetzblatt

Teil I

1939	Ausgegeben zu Berlin, den 13. Mai 1939	Nr. 90

209

Verordnung über den Reiseverkehr nach Spanien.
Vom 4. Mai 1939.

Auf Grund des Gesetzes über das Paß-, das Ausländerpolizei- und das Meldewesen sowie über das Ausweiswesen vom 11. Mai 1937 (Reichsgesetzbl. I S. 589) wird im Einvernehmen mit dem Reichsminister der Justiz folgendes verordnet:

§ 1

(1) Pässe von deutschen Staatsangehörigen mit Wohnsitz oder ständigem Aufenthalt im Inland sind für Reisen nach Spanien und nach den spanischen Besitzungen, einschließlich der Zone des spanischen Protektorats in Marokko, und für die Durchreise durch diese Gebiete bis auf weiteres nur gültig, wenn der Geltungsbereich des Passes durch einen entsprechenden Zusatz von der zuständigen Paßbehörde ausdrücklich auf diese Gebiete erstreckt ist.

(2) Der Zusatz über den Geltungsbereich des Passes für diese Gebiete lautet: „Gültig auch für Reisen nach und durch Spanien".

§ 2

Ein deutscher Staatsangehöriger, der ohne den nach dieser Verordnung erforderlichen Zusatz über den Geltungsbereich des Passes aus dem Reichsgebiet unmittelbar oder auf einem Umweg in oder durch die im § 1 Abs. 1 genannten Gebiete reist, wird mit Geldstrafe bestraft.

§ 3

Die Verordnung tritt mit dem Tag der Verkündung in Kraft. Gleichzeitig tritt die Verordnung zur Durchführung des Gesetzes zur Verhinderung der Teilnahme am spanischen Bürgerkrieg vom 20. Februar 1937 (Reichsgesetzbl. I S. 248) außer Kraft.

Berlin, den 4. Mai 1939.

Der Reichsminister des Innern

In Vertretung

H. Himmler

Verordnung zur Einführung des Gesetzes über Mietverhältnisse mit Juden in der Ostmark.
Vom 10. Mai 1939.

Auf Grund des § 14 des Gesetzes über Mietverhältnisse mit Juden vom 30. April 1939 (Reichsgesetzbl. I S. 864) wird verordnet:

Artikel 1

Das Gesetz über Mietverhältnisse mit Juden vom 30. April 1939 (Reichsgesetzbl. I S. 864) gilt in der Ostmark nach Maßgabe der folgenden Anpassungsvorschriften:

1. Zu § 1

§ 1 ist in folgender Fassung anzuwenden:

„(1) Ein Jude kann sich auf die dem Schutze der Mieter dienenden Vorschriften der §§ 19, 20, 22 und 23 des österreichischen Mietengesetzes (BGBl. Nr. 210/1929) nicht berufen, wenn der Vermieter bei der Kündigung eines Wohnraums durch eine Bescheinigung der Gemeindebehörde nachweist, daß für die Zeit nach der Beendigung des Mietverhältnisses die anderweitige Unterbringung des Mieters sichergestellt ist. Diese Bescheinigung ist dem Gericht bei der Anbringung der Kündigung vorzulegen.

(2) Betrifft die Kündigung nur andere Mietgegenstände als Wohnräume, so kann sich ein Jude auf die im Abs. 1 angeführten Vorschriften des Mietengesetzes überhaupt nicht berufen.

(3) Die Abs. 1 und 2 gelten nicht, wenn auch der Vermieter Jude ist."

2. Zu § 2

Bei der vorzeitigen Kündigung eines Mietverhältnisses gemäß § 2 des Gesetzes ist ohne Rücksicht auf die Dauer der gesetzlichen Kündigungsfrist eine Frist von drei Monaten einzuhalten. Die Kündigung muß spätestens am dritten Werktage eines Monats erfolgen und ist für den Schluß jedes Kalendermonats zulässig.

3. Zu § 3

Satz 2 des § 3 ist in folgender Fassung anzuwenden:

„Auf ein vertragliches Verbot der Untervermietung kann sich der Vermieter nicht berufen, wenn auch er Jude ist."

4. Zu § 9

§ 9 ist in folgender Fassung anzuwenden:

„(1) Ist nur der Mieter Jude, so darf ihm eine Verlängerung der Räumungsfrist nach den Vorschriften der §§ 38 bis 40 des österreichischen Mietengesetzes (BGBl. Nr. 210/1929) nur bewilligt werden, wenn er durch eine Bescheinigung der Gemeindebehörde nachweist, daß seiner anderweitigen Unterbringung Hindernisse entgegenstehen oder wenn die Räumung ohne ernstliche Schädigung der Gesundheit eines Betroffenen nicht durchführbar ist.

(2) § 575 Abs. 3 der österreichischen Zivilprozeßordnung gilt nicht, wenn nur der Mieter Jude ist."

5. Zu § 11

§ 11 ist in folgender Fassung anzuwenden:

„(1) Die Vorschriften dieses Gesetzes sind auch auf Kündigungen anzuwenden, die vor seinem Inkrafttreten bei Gericht angebracht worden sind. In diesen Fällen ist die in § 1 Abs. 1 geforderte Bescheinigung der Gemeindebehörde auch dann zu berücksichtigen, wenn sie erst im Rechtsmittelverfahren vorgelegt wird. Das Verfahren ist auf Antrag des Klägers zu unterbrechen, um ihm die Beibringung der Bescheinigung zu ermöglichen.

(2) Das Verfahren über Einwendungen gegen einen Räumungsauftrag, dessen Erlassung vor dem Inkrafttreten dieses Gesetzes beantragt worden ist, sowie das Verfahren über eine vor diesem Zeitpunkt angebrachte Klage auf Aufhebung eines Mietvertrages ist, wenn der Beklagte oder sein Ehegatte Jude ist, auf Antrag des Klägers zu unterbrechen, um ihm eine Kündigung nach den Vorschriften dieses Gesetzes zu ermöglichen.

(3) Das unterbrochene Verfahren ist auf Antrag des Klägers aufzunehmen.

(4) Wird die Kündigung wirksam oder erledigt sich der den Gegenstand des aufgeschobenen Verfahrens bildende Rechtsstreit dadurch, daß der Beklagte den Mietgegenstand räumt, so ist dem Beklagten auf Antrag des Klägers der Ersatz der Prozeßkosten des aufgeschobenen Verfahrens mit Beschluß aufzuerlegen."

Artikel 2

Das Gesetz über die Anforderung von Wohnungen und Geschäftsräumen (Gesetzbl. f. d. Land Österreich Nr. 588/1938) bleibt unberührt, soweit nicht die Vorschriften des § 4 des Gesetzes über Mietverhältnisse mit Juden Platz greifen.

Berlin, den 10. Mai 1939.

Der Reichsminister der Justiz
Dr. Gürtner

Der Reichsarbeitsminister
Franz Seldte

Der Reichsminister des Innern
In Vertretung
Dr. Stuckart

Verordnung zur Einführung des Gesetzes über Mietverhältnisse mit Juden in den sudetendeutschen Gebieten.
Vom 10. Mai 1939.

Auf Grund des § 14 des Gesetzes über Mietverhältnisse mit Juden vom 30. April 1939 (Reichsgesetzbl. I S. 864) wird verordnet:

Das Gesetz über Mietverhältnisse mit Juden vom 30. April 1939 (Reichsgesetzbl. I S. 864) gilt in den sudetendeutschen Gebieten nach Maßgabe der folgenden Anpassungsvorschriften:

1. Zu § 2

Bei der vorzeitigen Kündigung eines Mietverhältnisses gemäß § 2 des Gesetzes ist ohne Rücksicht auf die Dauer der gesetzlichen Kündigungsfrist eine Frist von drei Monaten einzuhalten. Die Kündigung muß spätestens am dritten Werktage eines Monats erfolgen und ist für den Schluß jedes Kalendermonats zulässig.

2. Zu § 3

Satz 2 ist in folgender Fassung anzuwenden:

„Auf ein vertragliches Verbot der Untervermietung kann sich der Vermieter nicht berufen, wenn auch er Jude ist."

3. Zu § 9

An die Stelle des § 9 tritt folgende Vorschrift:

„(1) Ist nur der Mieter Jude und ist die Kündigung bewilligt, so kommt ein Aufschub der exekutiven Räumung nur in Betracht, wenn der Mieter durch eine Bescheinigung der Gemeindebehörde nachweist, daß seiner anderweitigen Unterbringung Hindernisse entgegenstehen oder wenn die Räumung ohne erhebliche Schädigung der Gesundheit eines Betroffenen nicht durchführbar ist.

(2) § 575 Abs. 3 der Zivilprozeßordnung gilt nicht, wenn nur der Mieter Jude ist."

4. Zu § 11

§ 11 ist in folgender Fassung anzuwenden:

„Ist beim Inkrafttreten dieses Gesetzes gegen einen Juden oder den Ehegatten eines Juden ein Verfahren auf Bewilligung der Kündigung oder auf Räumung anhängig, so hat das Gericht auf Antrag des Klägers das Verfahren zu unterbrechen, um ihm die Kündigung nach den Vorschriften dieses Gesetzes zu ermöglichen. Erledigt sich der Rechtsstreit durch eine solche Kündigung, so sind die Gerichtskosten niederzuschlagen; die außergerichtlichen Kosten hat der Mieter zu tragen. Nimmt der Kläger die Klage zurück, so sind die Gerichtskosten niederzuschlagen und die außergerichtlichen Kosten gegeneinander aufzuheben."

Berlin, den 10. Mai 1939.

Der Reichsminister der Justiz
Dr. Gürtner

Der Reichsarbeitsminister
Franz Seldte

Der Reichsminister des Innern
In Vertretung
Dr. Stuckart

211

Bekanntmachung über das Außerkrafttreten des Gesetzes zur Verhinderung der Teilnahme am spanischen Bürgerkrieg und des Gesetzes über die Überwachung des Verkehrs der deutschen Handelsschiffahrt mit den spanischen Häfen.
Vom 4. Mai 1939.

Mit dem heutigen Tage treten außer Kraft:

1. das Gesetz zur Verhinderung der Teilnahme am spanischen Bürgerkrieg vom 18. Februar 1937 (Reichsgesetzbl. I S. 241);
2. das Gesetz über die Überwachung des Verkehrs der deutschen Handelsschiffahrt mit den spanischen Häfen vom 7. April 1937 (Reichsgesetzbl. II S. 127).

Diese Bekanntmachung ergeht auf Grund von § 5 des erstgenannten und von § 4 Abs. 2 des letztgenannten Gesetzes.

Berlin, den 4. Mai 1939.

Der Reichsminister des Auswärtigen
In Vertretung
Freiherr von Weizsäcker

Berichtigung

In der Vierten Verordnung zur Ausführung des Reichsjagdgesetzes vom 29. März 1939 (Reichsgesetzbl. I S. 643) müssen im Artikel 11 die Eingangsworte lauten: „Im § 37 erhalten die Sätze 5 und 6 des Absatzes 2 folgende Fassung:".

Berlin, den 10. Mai 1939.

Der Reichsjägermeister

Im Auftrag

Dr. Vollbach

Das Reichsgesetzblatt erscheint in zwei gesonderten Teilen — Teil I und Teil II —.
Fortlaufender Bezug nur durch die **Postanstalten**. Bezugspreis vierteljährlich für Teil I = 2,70 RM, für Teil II = 2,30 RM.
Einzelbezug jeder (auch jeder älteren) Nummer nur vom **Reichsverlagsamt**, Berlin NW 40, Scharnhorststraße Nr. 4 (Fernsprecher: 42 92 65 — Postscheckkonto: Berlin 962 00). Einzelnummern werden nach dem Umfang berechnet. Preis für den achtseitigen Bogen 15 Rpf, aus abgelaufenen Jahrgängen 10 Rpf, ausschließlich der Postdrucksachengebühr.
Bei größeren Bestellungen 10 bis 60 v. H. Preisermäßigung.
Herausgegeben vom Reichsministerium des Innern. — Gedruckt in der Reichsdruckerei, Berlin.